READY FOR INVALSI

✓ *Preparazione alla Prova Nazionale di INGLESE per la Scuola Secondaria di Primo grado*

✓ ***PROVE DISPONIBILI ANCHE IN VERSIONE DIGITALE* COMPUTER BASED**

GRUPPO EDITORIALE RAFFAELLO

celtic PUBLISHING

READY FOR INVALSI

La prova scritta INVALSI di lingua inglese ha lo scopo di misurare su tutto il territorio nazionale il livello di competenza di lingua inglese conseguito dagli studenti al termine del primo ciclo d'istruzione.
L'Istituto Nazionale per la valutazione del Sistema educativo d'Istruzione e formazione (INVALSI) intende valutare sia la competenza di lettura, intesa come capacità di comprendere e interpretare un testo scritto, sia le conoscenze linguistiche a livello lessicale e grammaticale, l'acquisizione delle quali è prevista nelle Indicazioni curriculari della Scuola Secondaria di Primo Grado.
Questo fascicolo ha lo scopo di aiutare gli studenti nella preparazione della prova INVALSI, facendo prendere loro dimestichezza con la tipologia della prova ed affrontarla quindi con sicurezza.
Il fascicolo è suddiviso in tre sezioni.
La prima parte - **Reading Comprehension** - presenta una serie graduata di 19 brani, autentici e non, di varia tipologia:
- 9 letture con attività di True/False/Doesn't say;
- 10 letture con quesiti a scelta multipla.

Ciascuna lettura pone dieci quesiti, strutturati in modo da valutare le competenze della capacità di lettura: la comprensione globale, l'individuazione di informazioni specifiche, l'intenzione comunicativa, lo scopo del testo, il genere a cui appartiene, l'individuazione del significato di lessico ed espressioni dal contesto.
La seconda parte - **Listening** - presenta una serie di ascolti calibrati sul modello Listening Cambridge Key (KET), 5 tipi di prove differenti, con ascolti online su www. raffaellodigitale.it.
La terza sezione - **Focus on Language and Grammar** - propone 14 schede di riflessione linguistica con quesiti a scelta multipla inerenti la conoscenza e l'uso della lingua inglese nei vari aspetti grammaticali, funzionali e lessicali.
I quesiti a scelta multipla prevedono 4 opzioni delle quali una sola è quella giusta e che dovrà essere contrassegnata con una crocetta sulla lettera corrispondente:

1 Completa la frase.
I ... play volleyball.
A am
~~**B**~~ can
C do
D can to

Nella pagina seguente vengono indicati alcuni suggerimenti utili per acquisire le strategie operative necessarie ad affrontare le tipologie della prova.

STRATEGIE PER AFFRONTARE UN TEST A SCELTA MULTIPLA

Il test di lettura a scelta multipla consente di verificare conoscenze, comprensione e capacità di analisi. Per ogni domanda vengono fornite quattro risposte, tutte plausibili, ma solo una esatta.

Reading Comprehension

- Leggi tutto il testo rapidamente prima di rispondere alle domande per farti un'idea generale del contenuto.
- Non preoccuparti delle parole che non conosci: puoi intuirne il significato dal resto della frase, ovvero dal contesto. Formula un'ipotesi sul significato e verifica se è coerente con il contenuto del messaggio.
- Leggi ogni singola domanda assicurandoti di aver ben capito cosa chiede. È necessario riconoscere/conoscere perfettamente il significato delle *Wh-question words: what, where, when, who, why, which, how, how often, how much, how many, how long, etc.*
- Leggi ogni singola opzione attentamente prima di scegliere la risposta: alcune domande possono avere quattro opzioni verosimili, è importante perciò leggerle tutte e quattro per scegliere la migliore risposta corretta.
- Rileggi il testo e cerca il paragrafo che contiene l'informazione utile alla scelta della risposta.
- Cerca nel testo spunti e suggerimenti che ti possono aiutare nella scelta: parole chiave, forme verbali, avverbi, negazioni.
- Se trovi difficile qualche quesito, usa la strategia dell'esclusione: considera ogni opzione una domanda vero/falso, elimina quelle che ritieni assolutamente sbagliate, in questo modo le probabilità di sbagliare risposta si riducono e puoi pensare alla risposta migliore.
- Dopo aver scelto la risposta, verifica nuovamente le opzioni rimaste con le informazioni nel testo per sincerarti che possano essere definitivamente scartate.

Focus on Language and Grammar

- Leggi attentamente la consegna e il contenuto della domanda.
- Ricorda che ciascun quesito si concentra su un solo aspetto grammaticale fra i tanti che hai studiato, per esempio:
  - uso dei tempi verbali
  - uso degli ausiliari
  - uso delle *Wh-question words*
  - parti del discorso (nome, verbo, aggettivo, articolo, avverbio, pronome, preposizioni, congiunzioni)
  - pronomi soggetto, pronomi complemento, pronomi possessivi, pronomi relativi
  - comparativi degli aggettivi (regolari-irregolari)
  - posizione degli avverbi
  - concordanze (tempo del verbo/espressioni di tempo)
  - forma passiva
  - discorso diretto/indiretto.
- Verifica nelle opzioni proposte quali errori di grammatica sono presenti in modo da escludere le proposte errate.
- Una volta fatta la scelta, riverificala chiedendoti: perché è giusta?

Indice

Reading Comprehension

Date:..

Don't panic!

For most students, taking exams can cause anxiety and getting ready for them can be very stressful. You may be afraid you are not good enough or haven't worked hard enough to pass them; you may feel the pressure of expectations from your family or your teachers. Don't panic! Proper studying techniques, planning ahead and smart time management skills are the key to minimizing that stress and helping you do your best.

Getting organised is the most important thing. You can't begin studying just a few weeks before the exam, you have to spread your studying over longer periods and make a timetable which includes every subject, allowing extra time for the difficult ones. Don't make a schedule that requires you to study six hours every day. Work out a plan to study about two hours per day and remember to take short breaks as soon as you notice you're losing concentration.

It's also important to select a comfortable place for studying, with the proper atmosphere where you can concentrate without being disturbed. Your plan should be flexible enough to include time for fun, relaxation and a healthy diet as well. Avoid fatty food, tea or fizzy drinks; food rich in vitamins and proteins, such as vegetables and fresh fruit, are a must because these nutrients help your brain stay sharp.

And don't forget that mind and body perform at their best if you get adequate rest, so sleep at least eight hours a night. On the day of the exam relax and do your best because your best is all that you can do! We are all different, achieve at different levels, and have different qualities and skills. Exam success depends on you. Be positive and don't panic!

expectations *aspettative*
ahead *in anticipo*
spread *distribuire*
allowing *concedendo*
requires *richiede*
sharp *attento, sveglio*

Indica se le affermazioni sono vere (True), false (False) o non menzionate (Doesn't say).

1 Exams are always stressful.	☒ True	☐ False	☐ Doesn't say
2 Family expectations can add to exam stress.	☒ True	☐ False	☐ Doesn't say
3 Your study plan should be prepared well in advance.	☒ True	☐ False	☐ Doesn't say
4 You have to study six hours a day.	☒ True	☐ False	☐ Doesn't say
5 You mustn't revise on Sundays.	☐ True	☐ False	☒ Doesn't say
6 It's a good idea to study continuously for 3 hours.	☐ True	☒ False	☐ Doesn't say
7 Physical activity is a good way to control exam stress.	☐ True	☐ False	☒ Doesn't say
8 You shouldn't eat crisps.	☐ True	☐ False	☒ Doesn't say
9 A good night's sleep is always very important.	☒ True	☐ False	☐ Doesn't say
10 If you follow this advice, you'll probably do well.	☒ True	☐ False	☐ Doesn't say

Date:..

Hairdryer safety instructions

READ BEFORE USING

- Always unplug a hairdryer when it is not being used. Even when it is switched off, the electricity has not been cut off.
- Do not use a hairdryer near or over water contained in baths, washbasins, sinks, etc.
- Do not place a hairdryer where it can fall into water.
- Never use a hairdryer while having a bath or a shower.
- Don't reach for a hairdryer if it falls into water or other liquid; unplug it immediately, and then remove it.
- Don't use a hairdryer outdoors.
- Never operate a hairdryer if it has a damaged cord or plug, if it is not working properly or if it has been dropped or damaged. Return it to a service centre for examination and repair.

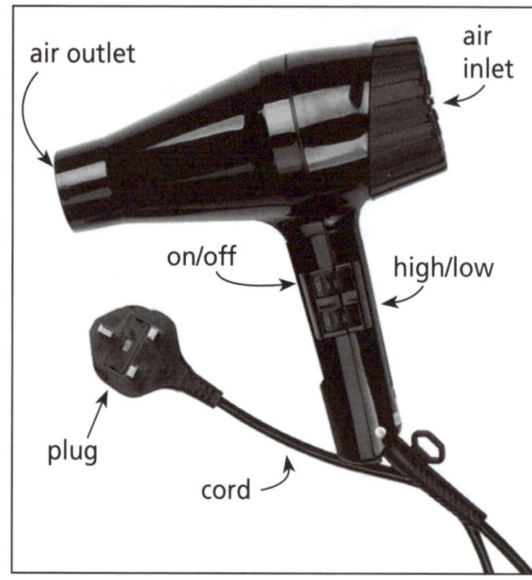

- If a hairdryer falls into water, do not use it again. Take it to an e-waste recycling centre.
- Check the condition of the cord regularly. Do not wind the cord around the hairdryer.
- Don't block the air inlet or outlet. Periodically check that the openings are free of fluff, hair or other matter. A hairdryer with blocked air openings may catch fire.

cut off *tagliare* **unplug** *staccare la spina* **wind** *avvolgere*

Indica se le affermazioni sono vere (True), false (False) o non menzionate (Doesn't say).

1	It is dangerous to leave a hairdryer plugged in.	☐ True	☐ False	☐ Doesn't say
2	The best place to keep a hairdryer is in a cupboard.	☐ True	☐ False	☐ Doesn't say
3	You can use a hairdryer while bathing.	☐ True	☐ False	☐ Doesn't say
4	Pull out the plug if a hairdryer falls into water.	☐ True	☐ False	☐ Doesn't say
5	Hairdryers can be used anywhere.	☐ True	☐ False	☐ Doesn't say
6	Children should not use hairdryers.	☐ True	☐ False	☐ Doesn't say
7	Service centres can fix broken cords.	☐ True	☐ False	☐ Doesn't say
8	If a hairdryer falls into water, it can be repaired.	☐ True	☐ False	☐ Doesn't say
9	Keep the cord away from heated surfaces.	☐ True	☐ False	☐ Doesn't say
10	A fire can start if the air inlet is blocked.	☐ True	☐ False	☐ Doesn't say

Date:..

Antarctica fact file

Name: The name Antarctica comes from the Greek word *Antarktikos*, meaning south of Arktos, the constellation known as Ursa Major, or the Great Bear, in the Northern Hemisphere. Since the ancient Greeks believed that the Earth was a sphere, it was logical that a landmass in the South balanced the world of the North.

Location: Antarctica is the southern-most continent on Earth surrounded by the Southern Ocean. The continent covers nearly 9% of the Earth's surface, and it is 25% bigger than Europe and double the size of Australia, making it the fifth largest continent after Asia, Africa, North and South America.

Land: 98% of the surface (14 million square kilometres) is covered with a vast ice sheet over 1.6 kilometres thick which represents the biggest resource of fresh water in the world. The remaining 2% is arid rock with mountains that range up to nearly 5,000 metres.

Natural resources: The main resources are coal, iron ore, oil and natural gas but none of them are extracted as the Antarctic Treaty (1959) preserves these resources and the ecosystem for strictly scientific purposes.

Climate: It is the windiest, driest and coldest continent with severe low temperatures (up to -89°C) and very low precipitation. Seasons are the opposite of the seasons in the Northern Hemisphere. The sun sets in March and rises in October.

Population: Because of the extreme weather conditions, there are no permanent inhabitants. The only people who live there are the staff from different countries who work at the scientific research stations.

Fauna: Antarctica has a few tiny land animals but a great number of marine animals, such as Emperor penguins, whales and seals.

balanced	*bilanciava*	**thick**	*spessa*	**sets**	*tramonta*
ice sheet	*lastra di ghiaccio*	**range up**	*elevano*	**rises**	*sorge*

Indica se le affermazioni sono vere (True), false (False) o non menzionate (Doesn't say).

1	The name 'Antarctica' derives from the word 'ant'.	☐ True	☐ False	☐ Doesn't say
2	Antarctica is at the North Pole.	☐ True	☐ False	☐ Doesn't say
3	Antarctica is half fertile land and half ice.	☐ True	☐ False	☐ Doesn't say
4	Antarctica is smaller than Australia.	☐ True	☐ False	☐ Doesn't say
5	It is the largest fresh water reserve on Earth.	☐ True	☐ False	☐ Doesn't say
6	Antarctica is not a flat country.	☐ True	☐ False	☐ Doesn't say
7	Gold is present in Antarctica.	☐ True	☐ False	☐ Doesn't say
8	There are 24 hours of light each day for six months.	☐ True	☐ False	☐ Doesn't say
9	The population is higher in January than in August.	☐ True	☐ False	☐ Doesn't say
10	The Emperor penguins are the tallest penguins.	☐ True	☐ False	☐ Doesn't say

Date:..

Stockholm: A European green capital

At a time when many of the world's great cities are facing chronic environmental problems, we need inspirational examples showing what cities can do to deal with them. Most of the environmental challenges facing our society happen in urban areas: and it is these areas that have the potential and the resources to bring together the commitment and generate the innovation needed to solve them.

We have to think beyond traditional problems. Caring for the urban environment doesn't just mean cutting CO_2 emissions. It also means thinking about the air we breathe, the water we drink and the noise that affects us. It means integrated long-term plans for the cities of tomorrow and the people who will live and work there. The European Green Capital Award promotes ideas such as sustainable mobility, modern waste management, sustainable land use, eco-innovation and other green technologies which drive towards sustainable development and more resource-efficient life. Stockholm met the challenge, winning the inaugural award in 2010.

Years of successful environmental work have turned Stockholm into one of the world's cleanest cities. More than 90% of the population lives within 300 metres of a green area, and the pure lake water, which makes up over 10% of Stockholm's surface area, is well-suited for the supply of drinking water. Just south of the city centre, the Hammarby Sjöstad residential area, which is still developing and is to be completed in 2015, is a perfect example of a sustainable city run on renewable sources: 100% of its household waste is converted into heating and electricity.

challenges *sfide*
commitment *impegno*
sustainable *rinnovabile*
drive towards *conducono a*
supply *fornitura*
heating *riscaldamento*

Indica se le affermazioni sono vere (True), false (False) o non menzionate (Doesn't say).

1 The 21st century is facing environmental challenges. ☐ True ☐ False ☐ Doesn't say
2 Urban areas are growing. ☐ True ☐ False ☐ Doesn't say
3 CO_2 emissions cause environmental problems. ☐ True ☐ False ☐ Doesn't say
4 The European Green Capital Award is a global initiative. ☐ True ☐ False ☐ Doesn't say
5 The first European Green Capital Award was given in 2010. ☐ True ☐ False ☐ Doesn't say
6 90% of Stockholm's surface area is water. ☐ True ☐ False ☐ Doesn't say
7 Water in Stockholm is polluted. ☐ True ☐ False ☐ Doesn't say
8 Waste is damaging the environment in Stockholm. ☐ True ☐ False ☐ Doesn't say
9 Hammarby will be energy self-sufficient by 2015. ☐ True ☐ False ☐ Doesn't say
10 Sustainable cities are based on renewable resources. ☐ True ☐ False ☐ Doesn't say

Date:..

A holiday diary

Tuesday 13th August.

What a day! We left home at 7.30 this morning to drive the 20 kms to the airport. After 10 kms, Dad realised that he had left the tickets on the kitchen table. Total panic! We returned home, Dad ran into the house, grabbed the tickets and then drove like the wind back to the airport. Luckily our flight was delayed by half an hour so we had a little time to relax before checking in.

The flight was uneventful although Ted was very excited because it was his first time on a plane. The flight attendant served us snacks and some orange juice and before I knew it, we were landing in Barcelona.

It was hot and sunny when we finally got out of the airport. We found a taxi to take us to our hotel. I said 'Gracias', my first word in Spanish, to the driver when he put our bags in the boot. He replied,'De nada', which Dad told me means, 'You're welcome'.

The hotel is fab, there's an enormous TV and a docking station for my mp3 player in our room. After unpacking, we all went down to the pool. Ted and I played in the water while Mum and Dad relaxed and sunbathed. We met two German boys, Klaus and Werner, who are about our ages and speak English. They're really nice! Klaus taught me a few German words but it's very difficult! I think he has a crush on me!

In the evening Mum and Dad took us to 'La Locanda', a restaurant in the hotel. It was an amazing place. They serve food from all over the world, from fish and chips to curry, hamburgers and lasagne. Mum insisted that we eat Spanish food because we are in Spain so I had a delicious rice and fish dish called paella. Yummy! Ted didn't like his spicy sausage called chorizo but he's never been very adventurous with food. Well, that's all for now!

¡Hasta mañana! That's Spanish for 'See you tomorrow!'.

grabbed *afferrò* **landing** *atterrando* **a crush on me** *una cotta per me*
uneventful *senza intoppi* **sunbathed** *prendevano il sole*

Indica se le affermazioni sono vere (True), false (False) o non menzionate (Doesn't say).

1 They took the bus to the airport.	☐ True	☐ False	☐ Doesn't say
2 Dad forgot the airline tickets.	☐ True	☐ False	☐ Doesn't say
3 The flight was on time.	☐ True	☐ False	☐ Doesn't say
4 It was the family's first holiday abroad.	☐ True	☐ False	☐ Doesn't say
5 The plane didn't take off from Barcelona.	☐ True	☐ False	☐ Doesn't say
6 The taxi driver can speak English.	☐ True	☐ False	☐ Doesn't say
7 They can listen to music in their room.	☐ True	☐ False	☐ Doesn't say
8 Klaus and Werner are older than Ted.	☐ True	☐ False	☐ Doesn't say
9 Ted likes trying different food.	☐ True	☐ False	☐ Doesn't say
10 The writer of the diary is a boy.	☐ True	☐ False	☐ Doesn't say

Date:..

Great Barrier Reef in danger

A new study, by the Australian Institute of Marine Science (AIMS), shows that The Great Barrier Reef, the world's largest living organism covering an area of about 345,000 square kilometres off the coast of north-east Australia, has lost more than half its coral in the past three decades. Coral loss has been running at about 0.53% annually since 1985, with most of the damage occurring in the southern regions while the relatively pristine northern region is quite stable.

Scientists from the Institute report that intense tropical cyclones and periodic population explosions of crown-of-thorns starfish are mostly to blame for the devastating loss of coral at this World Heritage Site. Coral bleaching, resulting from ocean warming, has a minor role in coral loss. Jamie Oliver, an AIMS scientist, says reducing the population of crown-of-thorns starfish that feed on the coral is the best way to prevent further destruction to the reef.

'We believe that if we take action on one of the things we can directly control, the crown-of-thorns starfish, it may leave the reef in a position where it can better withstand some of these climatic impacts, such as cyclones and coral bleaching,' said Oliver.

The study also shows that monitoring global climate change and water temperatures around the reef is essential for its future. Without intervention, the amount of coral could halve again by 2022.

pristine *incontaminato*
crown-of-thorns starfish *stella marina corona di spine*
to blame for *essere responsabile di*
bleaching *sbiancamento*
withstand *resistere*
halve *dimezzare*

Indica se le affermazioni sono vere (True), false (False) o non menzionate (Doesn't say).

1 The Reef has been in danger for about thirty years. ☐ True ☐ False ☐ Doesn't say
2 Cyclones have a risky impact on the reef. ☐ True ☐ False ☐ Doesn't say
3 All species of marine life damage the coral reef. ☐ True ☐ False ☐ Doesn't say
4 Ocean warming is the main cause of coral loss. ☐ True ☐ False ☐ Doesn't say
5 Crown-of-thorns starfish cause the reef's whitening. ☐ True ☐ False ☐ Doesn't say
6 Crown-of-thorns starfish eat coral. ☐ True ☐ False ☐ Doesn't say
7 Crown-of-thorns starfish are poisonous. ☐ True ☐ False ☐ Doesn't say
8 Cooler water temperatures may resolve coral loss. ☐ True ☐ False ☐ Doesn't say
9 Damage to the coral reef can be prevented. ☐ True ☐ False ☐ Doesn't say
10 There will be no more coral left in 2022. ☐ True ☐ False ☐ Doesn't say

Date:...

The festival capital of the world

Edinburgh is not only the capital of Scotland, it is also the festival capital of the world! Every year more than four million people go to at least one of the arts and culture festivals held in this dynamic and fascinating medieval city. Summer is the peak season when eight of its twelve festivals take place. Perhaps the two best-known summer festivals are the prestigious Edinburgh International Festival (EIF) and the casually cool Edinburgh Fringe Festival (The Fringe). Both festivals, held for three weeks in August, are extraordinary celebrations of the performing arts.

The EIF was founded in 1947 as a post-war initiative to re-unite Europe and the world through culture and the arts. Sir Rudolf Bing, the first Festival Director, when planning the programme for the inaugural festival was determined to make it an unforgettable and powerful event; he wanted the EIF to 'embrace the world' and heal the wounds caused by the war. For more than six decades, on the invitation of the EIF Director, world class artists and musicians have continued to offer audiences unforgettable and powerful performances of classical music, theatre, opera and dance.

The Fringe also started in the same year as the EIF. It was established as an alternative festival by the many artists and musicians who had not been invited to perform at the EIF, but arrived all the same and performed in the streets of the city. Its founding principle - an arts festival open to anybody who wants to perform - is still as relevant today as it was in 1947. The Fringe is the largest arts festival in the world featuring theatre, children's shows, exhibitions, dance, music and comedy. It is a very important international platform for both known and unknown artists who want to develop and build their career. At the 2012 festival, 42,096 performances were given in 279 locations by 22,457 performers from over 47 countries.

peak *di massima importanza* **heal the wounds** *guarire le ferite* **principle** *principio*

Indica se le affermazioni sono vere (True), false (False) o non menzionate (Doesn't say).

1 The population of Scotland is four million. ☐ True ☐ False ☐ Doesn't say
2 Edinburgh hosts twelve festivals every summer. ☐ True ☐ False ☐ Doesn't say
3 The Edinburgh Film Festival is in June. ☐ True ☐ False ☐ Doesn't say
4 The EIF began after the Second World War. ☐ True ☐ False ☐ Doesn't say
5 Sir Rudolf Bing was born in Scotland. ☐ True ☐ False ☐ Doesn't say
6 Artists have to be invited to perform at EIF. ☐ True ☐ False ☐ Doesn't say
7 Both the EIF and the Fringe were founded in 1947. ☐ True ☐ False ☐ Doesn't say
8 Anyone can perform at the Fringe. ☐ True ☐ False ☐ Doesn't say
9 The Fringe is just for young unknown artists. ☐ True ☐ False ☐ Doesn't say
10 Foreign artists have always come to the Fringe. ☐ True ☐ False ☐ Doesn't say

Reading Comprehension 8

Date:..

An Aesop's fable retold

Hare didn't have any friends because he was a bully. He was always making fun of the animals that were not as good-looking or as fast as he was. One fine day, while jogging through the forest, Hare saw Tortoise who was having a rest under a tree. He started bullying Tortoise, 'Look at those little legs and those ugly feet! You are the slowest animal I know!'

Tortoise was hurt by Hare's words and said, 'Well, maybe I am slow but I get where I have to go just as you do!'

Hare burst out laughing and shouted, 'Yes, but I always get where I am going faster than you or anyone else. Not even Usain Bolt can beat me.'

Tortoise decided to teach the bully a lesson, so he responded, 'Cool! Let's have a race! I'll show you that slow and sure is better than fast and careless!'

Hare accepted the challenge. Tortoise asked Fox to mark out the course for the race. All the animals came to watch. As soon as Fox called out, 'Ready, steady, go!', Hare took off like a bolt of lightning. Halfway through the race, he turned round to see if there was any sign of Tortoise. Of course there wasn't, so he decided to take a little nap. After an hour, Hare woke up and started running again. Hare was shocked as he approached the finishing line and saw Tortoise already on the other side being congratulated by all the animals.

'Oh no! I've lost! That's impossible!' he screamed.

Tortoise smiled at Hare and softly said, 'Nothing is impossible! Slow and sure is the best way to do anything!'

hare *lepre*
making fun *prendeva in giro*
tortoise *tartaruga*
burst out laughing *scoppiò a ridere*
mark out *delimitare*
took off *partì*

Indica se le affermazioni sono vere (True), false (False) o non menzionate (Doesn't say).

1 Hare always had fun with the other animals. ☐ True ☐ False ☐ Doesn't say
2 Hare met Tortoise in the forest on a summer day. ☐ True ☐ False ☐ Doesn't say
3 Tortoise was the slowest animal in the forest. ☐ True ☐ False ☐ Doesn't say
4 Hare offended Tortoise. ☐ True ☐ False ☐ Doesn't say
5 Hare said Usain Bolt wasn't as fast as he was. ☐ True ☐ False ☐ Doesn't say
6 Hare challenged Tortoise to a race. ☐ True ☐ False ☐ Doesn't say
7 Fox ran in the race. ☐ True ☐ False ☐ Doesn't say
8 Tortoise saw Hare having a rest during the race. ☐ True ☐ False ☐ Doesn't say
9 Hare didn't see Tortoise cross the finish line. ☐ True ☐ False ☐ Doesn't say
10 Slow but sure is as good as fast and careless. ☐ True ☐ False ☐ Doesn't say

My hero

From: lisa@myemail.az
To: jack@youremail.az
Subject: Help!

Hi Jack,

How are you? I am really busy with a History assignment and I need your help.
Yesterday in History class, we had a discussion about who our heroes were and why. Everyone named someone who wasn't alive: Churchill, Amelia Earhart, Steve Jobs and so on. When my teacher asked me who my hero was, the bell rang! Thank goodness, as I couldn't think of anyone who hadn't already been mentioned. But then my teacher told me to choose a hero, someone who hadn't already been talked about, and to prepare an oral presentation for the class on what he/she achieved and why he/she was my hero, for Monday.
So last night, while I was doing the washing up, I started thinking about modern day heroes, you know, heroes who are alive today. Then mum turned on the TV and I saw my hero... Alex Zanardi.
Here's what I am going to say on Monday! Could you read it and tell me what you think?

Alex Zanardi is not only a great sportsman, but also an incredible individual who has overcome adversity in his life. He was born in Bologna and started racing karts when he was thirteen. Later he went on to compete in Formula One racing. But in 2001, he was in an F1 crash which resulted in the amputation of his legs. Most people would have stopped racing and thought their life and career were over, but not Alex! He looked to the positive and began walking again shortly after the accident. Then, he returned to racing, and in 2010 he took up hand cycling. At the 2012 London Paralympics he won a gold medal in hand cycling. Alex is my hero because he is an inspiring figure of determination, sportsmanship and humility. He has shown the world that life is a precious gift and it is possible to achieve anything.

Call me after you read this @! Thanks a million!
Lisa

Indica se le affermazioni sono vere (True), false (False) o non menzionate (Doesn't say).

1 Lisa is a middle school student. ☐ True ☐ False ☐ Doesn't say
2 Her classmates talked about heroes from the past. ☐ True ☐ False ☐ Doesn't say
3 The bell rang after Lisa answered her teacher. ☐ True ☐ False ☐ Doesn't say
4 Mum helped her with her assignment. ☐ True ☐ False ☐ Doesn't say
5 Lisa chose a modern day hero. ☐ True ☐ False ☐ Doesn't say
6 Alex Zanardi won some Formula One races. ☐ True ☐ False ☐ Doesn't say
7 Zanardi lost his legs in a kart race. ☐ True ☐ False ☐ Doesn't say
8 He was determined to race again after the accident. ☐ True ☐ False ☐ Doesn't say
9 Lisa saw Zanardi on TV win at the 2012 Olympics. ☐ True ☐ False ☐ Doesn't say
10 Jack rang Lisa after reading the e-mail. ☐ True ☐ False ☐ Doesn't say

Date:...

Leggi il testo e scegli la risposta corretta.

Foreigners and the Italian language

Everyone knows that in today's world speaking at least one if not two foreign languages is important as it gives you the ability to communicate with a greater number of people. Mandarin Chinese, Spanish, English, Hindi and Arabic are the most widely-spoken languages in the world, whereas English, Spanish, Mandarin Chinese, Japanese and Arabic are those most studied. As incredible as it may seem, even Italian, with only about 60 million native speakers, is also one of the most studied foreign languages in the world. In fact, in the USA and the UK it is the fourth most studied language and the second in Canada! But, why are foreigners studying Italian?

Some foreigners study Italian because they want to learn the language of the country which, from the 13th to the 16th centuries, was not only the wealthiest one in Europe but also the centre of banking, science, philosophy, painting and sculpture, and world exploration. They know that if they speak and read Italian, they can have a better understanding of the history, art, music, and literature of one of the most beautiful countries in the world.

Others are keen on speaking Italian because they are planning a holiday to Italy. With 45 UNESCO World Heritage Sites and over 40% of the cultural riches of the world, about 45 million people visit Italy every year. Many of these holidaymakers study Italian because during their travels they want to talk and listen to the people, and learn about Italy's traditions and food.

Still others are interested in learning Italian because someone in their family emigrated from Italy. In fact, between 1861 and 1976, over 26 million Italians left Italy and moved to other countries in Europe, North and South America, and Australia. Today many of the 80 million descendants of those men and women who emigrated decades ago, are now studying the Italian language so they can identify, understand and connect with their Italian heritage.

whereas *mentre*
World Heritage Site *patrimonio culturale mondiale*
riches *ricchezze*
Italian heritage *radici italiane*

1 **According to the text, why is it important to learn foreign languages?**
A To be able to do business in China.
B To be able to use the internet.
C To be able to speak to people.
D To be able to go to Spain.

2 **Which language is less widely-spoken?**
A Mandarin Chinese.
B English.
C Arabic.
D Japanese.

3 **In which country is Italian the second most studied foreign language?**
A China.
B Canada.
C The United States.
D The United Kingdom.

4 **What does the phrase 'the wealthiest one' mean? [line 10]**
A It means the most populated country.
B It means the smallest country.
C It means the richest country.
D It means the biggest country.

5 **One of the reasons why people study Italian is to better understand...**
A Italian scientific experiments.
B Italian explorers.
C Italian literature.
D Italian banks.

6 **Who are 'holidaymakers'? [line 16]**
A People who are tour operators.
B People who have holiday homes.
C People who travel during Christmas holidays.
D People who travel for pleasure.

7 **About how many Italians immigrated to another country in the 19th and 20th centuries?**
A Twenty-six million.
B Forty-five million.
C Sixty million.
D Eighty million.

8 **Which country did the Italians NOT immigrate to?**
A The USA.
B Australia.
C Italy.
D Canada.

9 **Why do you think people who are of Italian heritage study the language?**
A To communicate with their ancestors in Italy.
B To understand where they come from.
C To learn about Italy.
D To enjoy Italian food.

10 **What is the purpose of this text?**
A To encourage people to visit Italy.
B To explain why people study Italian.
C To recommend people study Italian.
D To inform people about foreign languages.

Date:..

Leggi il testo e scegli la risposta corretta.

The Story of Dr Dolittle: Chapter 1 - Puddleby

Once upon a time, many years ago when our grandfathers were little children - there was a doctor; and his name was Dolittle - John Dolittle, MD. 'MD' means that he was a proper doctor and knew a whole lot.

He lived in a little town called, Puddleby-on-the-Marsh. All the folks, young and old, knew him well by sight. And whenever he walked down the street in his high hat everyone would say, 'There goes the Doctor! - He's a clever man.' And the dogs and the children would all run up and follow behind him; and even the crows that lived in the church-tower would caw and nod their heads.

The house he lived in, on the edge of the town, was quite small; but his garden was very large and had a wide lawn and stone seats and weeping-willows hanging over. His sister, Sarah Dolittle, was housekeeper for him; but the Doctor looked after the garden himself.

He was very fond of animals and kept many kinds of pets. Besides the gold-fish in the pond at the bottom of his garden, he had rabbits in the pantry, white mice in his piano, a squirrel in the linen closet and a hedgehog in the cellar. He had a cow with a calf too, and an old lame horse - twenty-five years of age - and chickens, and pigeons, and two lambs, and many other animals. But his favorite pets were Dab-Dab the duck, Jip the dog, Gub-Gub the baby pig, Polynesia the parrot, and the owl Too-Too.

His sister used to grumble about all these animals and said they made the house untidy. And one day when an old lady with rheumatism came to see the Doctor, she sat on the hedgehog who was sleeping on the sofa and never came to see him any more, but drove every Saturday all the way to Oxenthorpe, another town ten miles off, to see a different doctor.

crows *cornacchie*
caw *gracchiare*
nod *fare cenno*
lawn *prato*
weeping-willows *salici piangenti*
pantry *dispensa*
lame *zoppo*
grumble *brontolare*
hedgehog *riccio*

1 **When does the story take place?**
A A couple of years ago.
B A long time ago.
C In the early 1970s.
D About twenty-five years ago.

2 **In line 2, the acronym MD stands for...**
A managing director.
B master's degree.
C medical dentist.
D medical doctor.

3 **Which sentence has the same meaning as the sentence 'All folks, young and old, knew him well by sight.'? [lines 4-5]**
A Everybody liked him very much.
B Everybody always saw him in town.
C Everybody knew who he was.
D Everybody knew him very well.

4 **What does the phrase 'a clever man' mean? [line 6]**
A A man who is intelligent.
B A man who wears elegant clothes.
C A man who isn't very rich.
D A man who everyone likes.

5 **Where did Dr Doolittle live?**
A In a big city near Puddleby-on-the-Marsh.
B In the historic centre of a small village.
C On the outskirts of town.
D Near the church on the high street.

6 **Dr Dolittle lived in...**
A a small flat with a big garden.
B a big flat with a small garden.
C a little house with a small garden.
D a little house with a big garden.

7 **What did Sarah Dolittle do?**
A She was a doctor.
B She was Dr Dolittle's sister.
C She looked after her brother's house.
D She took care of her brother's garden.

8 **Which statement is FALSE?**
A Lots of animals lived in Dr Dolittle's house.
B Dr Dolittle didn't have any birds as pets.
C Dr Dolittle had five favourite pets.
D Dr Dolittle had a great love for animals.

9 **Why do you think the old woman changed doctors?**
A Because Dr Dolittle kept animals in his house.
B Because she lived closer to Oxenthorpe.
C Because Dr Doolittle couldn't cure her.
D Because she had rheumatism.

10 **The author wrote this text to...**
A update readers on the developments of pet therapy.
B persuade readers that animals are funny.
C entertain readers with a funny story about animals.
D tell readers about the difficulties of being a doctor.

Date:...

Leggi il testo e scegli la risposta corretta.

Bikes are back!

Italians have always loved cars: big ones, small ones, sleek luxury ones, tiny compact ones. In fact, with a population of a little over 60 million, Italy has one of the highest car ownership rates in the world: 600 cars for every 1,000 people. However, times are changing and Italy's love for cars in the 21st century may be ending as the bicycle is slowly making a comeback.

In 2011 sales figures showed that bicycles outsold cars for the first time since the Second World War - 1,750,000 bicycles were bought compared to 1,748,000 cars. The reasons bike sales are up and car sales are down in Italy are because of the recent high cost of petrol, the rise in unemployment and the increase in the cost of living. Consequently, many families have started to think twice before buying a new car or even using the one they have and lots of Italians are beginning to swap their four wheels for two as their preferred mode of transportation.

Bike riding offers many advantages and benefits over car travel. Besides being a great way to save money on petrol and car parking costs, it is also an easy way to keep fit and to save time. Travelling by car on the narrow and crowded streets in the historic city centres of Italy, especially during working hours when traffic is often intense and chaotic, can be quite stressful and time-consuming. Studies show that at rush hour the fastest way to travel five kilometres in the heart of any big Italian city is not by car, by bus or by taxi but by bike.

Currently there are 6.5 million Italians who commute to and from work and school by bicycle every day, while another 15 million ride bicycles at the weekends. These numbers are destined to grow as more and more people become aware of the negative impact cars have on the environment. Cars produce an enormous amount of greenhouse gases and smog-causing pollutants which are responsible for global warming and numerous heart and respiratory diseases. By understanding the advantages and benefits of bike riding to people and to the planet, perhaps a new renaissance, a cycling renaissance, may soon take place in Italy!

sleek *eleganti*
ownership *proprietà*
comeback *ritorno*
sales figures *dati di vendita*
outsold *superato nelle vendite*
unemployment *disoccupazione*
swap *scambiare*
rush hour *ora di punta*
commute *fare la spola*
become aware of *si rende conto di*
renaissance *rinascita*

1 **What does the term 'car ownership rates' refer to? [line 3]**
A It refers to the cost of cars in Italy.
B It refers to the number of cars sold in Italy.
C It refers to the number of cars owned in Italy.
D It refers to the number of cars on the road in Italy.

2 **How many more bicycles than cars were bought in Italy in 2011?**
A 1,750,000
B 1,748,000
C 2,000
D 600

3 **Which factor is NOT responsible for the recent drop in car sales in Italy?**
A The increase in population.
B The increase in the cost of living.
C The increase in unemployment.
D High petrol prices.

4 **Which phrase best substitutes the following 'Italians are beginning to swap their four wheels for two'? [line 11]**
A Italians are starting to sell their cars for motorcycles.
B Italians are starting to trade in their cars for bicycles.
C Italians are starting to exchange four cars for two cars.
D Italians are starting to switch from their bicycles to cars.

5 **Which statement about the bicycle is FALSE?**
A Bicycles keep you healthy.
B You do not have to pay for petrol.
C You do not save money by bicycling.
D Travelling by bike can save time.

6 **Streets in most historic city centres in Italy during rush hour are...**
A quiet and crowded.
B very wide and full of people and cars.
C intense and chaotic.
D quiet and stressful.

7 **According to the text, which would be the quickest way to do a five-kilometre journey if you were in the centre of Rome?**
A Walking.
B Driving a car.
C Calling a taxi.
D Riding a bicycle.

8 **The percentage of Italians who use a bike every day is about...**
A 6.5%
B 10%
C 15%
D 65%

9 **Why do cars have a negative impact on the environment?**
A Because they are expensive.
B Because they are faster than bicycles.
C Because they do not emit greenhouse gases.
D Because they pollute the air.

10 **The purpose of this text is...**
A to encourage people to buy a bicycle.
B to explain why Italians love their cars.
C to inform people about an alternative means of transport.
D to warn people about the dangers of greenhouse gases.

Date:...

Leggi il testo e scegli la risposta corretta.

Vitamin D-Quick Facts

What is vitamin D and what does it do?
Vitamin D is a nutrient found in some foods that is needed for health and to maintain strong bones.
It does so by helping the body absorb calcium (one of the main building blocks of bones) from food and supplements. People who get too little vitamin D may develop soft, thin, and brittle bones, a condition known as rickets in children, and osteomalacia.
Vitamin D is important to the body in many other ways as well. Muscles need it to move, nerves need it to carry messages between the brain and every body part, and the immune system needs vitamin D to fight off invading bacteria and viruses. Together with calcium, vitamin D also helps protect older adults from osteoporosis. Vitamin D is found in cells throughout the body.

Can I get vitamin D from the sun?
The body makes vitamin D when skin is directly exposed to the UV sun rays, and most people meet at least some of their vitamin D needs this way. Skin exposed to sunshine indoors through a window will not produce vitamin D. Cloudy days, shade, and having dark-coloured skin also cut down on the amount of vitamin D the skin makes.
However, despite the importance of the sun to vitamin D synthesis, it is prudent to limit exposure of skin to sunlight in order to lower the risk of skin cancer. When out in the sun for more than a few minutes, wear protective clothing and apply sunscreen with a high SPF (sun protection factor).
People who avoid the sun or who cover their bodies with sunscreen or clothing should include good sources of vitamin D in their diets or take a supplement.

How much vitamin D do I need?
The amount of vitamin D you need each day depends on your age. Average daily recommended amounts from the Food and Nutrition Board (an American group of experts) for different ages are listed in the table below, in International Units (IU):

Life Stage	Recommended Amount
Birth to 12 months	400 IU
Children 1–13 years	600 IU
Teens 14–18 years	600 IU
Adults 19–70 years	600 IU
Adults 71 years +++	800 IU
Pregnant and breastfeeding women	600 IU

What foods provide vitamin D?
Very few foods naturally have vitamin D. Fatty fish such as salmon, tuna, and mackerel are among the best sources, whereas cheese and egg yolks provide small amounts. Many breakfast cereals and some brands of orange juice, yogurt, margarine, and soya beverages are fortified with vitamin D in order to provide the recommended intake of the nutrient.

supplement *integrazione*
rickets *rachitismo*
fight off *combattere*
throughout *in tutto*
UV sun rays *raggi ultravioletti*
meet *soddisfare*
shade *ombra*
cut down on *ridurre*
average *medio*
IU *UI (0.025 microgrammi)*
mackerel *sgombro*
intake *assunzione*

1 **Why do we need vitamin D?**
A To absorb magnesium.
B To absorb calcium.
C To absorb water.
D To absorb food.

2 **What does the term 'brittle bones' mean? [line 9]**
A Strong bones.
B Fragile bones.
C Old bones.
D Green bones.

3 **What is NOT true about vitamin D?**
A It is unnecessary for the immune system.
B It is necessary for bones.
C It is necessary for muscles.
D It helps protect from bacteria.

4 **How is vitamin D made?**
A From sugar.
B From water.
C From sunlight.
D From blood.

5 **Which statement about vitamin D is TRUE?**
A Vitamin D is produced by the exposure of the skin to infrared light.
B Vitamin D is produced by the exposure of the skin to ultraviolet light.
C Vitamin D isn't produced by the exposure of the skin to ultraviolet light.
D Vitamin D is produced by the exposure of the skin to shade.

6 **What can cause vitamin D deficiency?**
A Wearing clothes that cover most of your body.
B Spending time outdoors.
C Having fair skin.
D Eating oily fish.

7 **The daily recommended amount of vitamin D depends...**
A on how tall you are.
B on how old you are.
C on how much you weigh.
D on whether you are male or female.

8 **According to the table, vitamin D intake for teenagers is...**
A less than new born babies.
B more than people over 71.
C less than children aged 10.
D the same as adults under 71.

9 **Where can you naturally find vitamin D?**
A In a lot of foods.
B In no foods.
C In all types of fish.
D In a very limited number of foods.

10 **What is the purpose of this text?**
A To promote brands of breakfast cereals.
B To tell people about SPFs.
C To inform people about the importance of vitamin D.
D To persuade people to eat fatty fish.

Date:..

Leggi il testo e scegli la risposta corretta.

Curriculum Vitae: Marc Rouge

Professional Profile

A dedicated and responsible travel consultant with vast experience in organising and managing promotional events, workshops and trade fairs in Europe and the USA.

Objective

I am looking for a challenging new position in a large multinational company in the tourist industry in Japan.

Career Summary

02/2011 - present
Executive Travel Consultant
Open Road Travel and Logistics, London, UK

- In charge of the daily operations of the office.
- Organise special events and trade fairs.
- Maintain a vast network of contacts with travel agencies, trade associations and educational institutions.
- Manage the company's website content.

07/2009 - 01/2011
Cross Cultural Trainer
Global Movement Solutions Company, New York, USA

- Organised educational programmes and workshops.
- Conducted cross-cultural training seminars.
- Planned and developed travel catalogues for the American, French, Italian and German markets.

Education

2005 - 2009
Nouvelle Université, Paris, France
Degree in Economics & Management of Tourism.

Languages

French	- Mother tongue
English	- Excellent verbal and written communication skills. - Living in English speaking countries since 2009.
Italian	- Good verbal and written communication skills. - Lived in Milan 6 years.

Experience and skills

Extensive travel in Europe, the USA, and Argentina.
Computer skills: Microsoft Word, Excel, PowerPoint.

1 **What is a 'professional profile'? [line 1]**
A A face profile that looks very professional.
B A job in the tourism sector.
C A description of one's qualifications and strengths.
D Information about one's friends and family.

2 **What does Marc Rouge do?**
A He works as a travel agent.
B He works in the travel industry.
C He goes to special events.
D He is a business consultant.

3 **Where does Marc Rouge want to work?**
A In London.
B In Europe.
C In Japan.
D In the States.

4 **Which is one of Marc Rouge's responsibilities at Open Road Travel and Logistics?**
A To attend travel events.
B To create websites for the company.
C To set up educational programmes.
D To supervise day to day operations in the office.

5 **What does the phrase 'maintain a vast network of contacts' mean? [line 11]**
A To be in charge of a big television network.
B To stay connected with lots of people.
C To keep a lot of people working.
D To watch lots of TV programmes.

6 **How long did he work as a Cross Cultural Trainer?**
A For nineteen months.
B Since July 2009.
C Since January 2011.
D For two years.

7 **Marc Rouge...**
A has a degree in History.
B finished university in 2005.
C received a master in Economics.
D got his degree in 2009.

8 **Which language do you think Marc speaks the best?**
A Japanese.
B English.
C French.
D Italian.

9 **According to the text, Marc lived in...**
A England, the USA and Canada.
B Argentina, England and Germany.
C England, the USA and Japan.
D Italy, the USA and France.

10 **Why do you think Marc wrote his curriculum vitae?**
A To find a better job abroad.
B To do some travelling in Japan.
C To see how much experience he has.
D To find a job in a Japanese computer company.

Date:..

Leggi il testo e scegli la risposta corretta.

The Shard of Glass: A vertical city

Ever since the start of the 21st century, there has been a boom in the construction of skyscrapers in London. The most recent tall tower to appear on the capital's skyline is called 'The Shard'. It was completed in April 2012 and officially opened to the public on 5th July 2012. For a lot of Londoners this bold architectural addition is the greatest and most beautiful sky-reaching building to be erected in London since the completion of the new St Paul's Cathedral in 1710.

The Shard was designed by the famous Italian architect Renzo Piano in the year 2000. Mr Piano took his inspiration from the tall sailing ships that once populated the River Thames and from the spires of London's churches especially from those of St Paul's Cathedral, which was designed by the English architect Sir Christopher Wren.

Renzo Piano wanted to design something different, not just another tall, anonymous office block. His vision was to create a 'vertical city': one mega-structure with places where people could work, shop, eat, live and enjoy themselves. So he designed the Shard, a 'vertical city' inside an 87-storey, pyramid-shaped glass and steel skyscraper.

This spectacular building reaches 310 metres into the sky. It is the tallest structure in London. It is 214m taller than Big Ben, 199m taller than St Paul's Cathedral, 131m taller than Nelson's Column in Trafalgar Square, and 21m taller than the BT (British Telecom) Tower.

The 11,000 glass panels, which cover the sides of the skyscraper, reflect sunlight and the sky. Hence, the colour and the aspect of the Shard change according to the weather and the seasons. There are 72 habitable levels and a further 15 levels which make up the slender spire at the top of the skyscraper. 44 lifts take you up to the building's offices and shops, piazzas and winter gardens, cafés and international restaurants, five-star luxury hotel with a swimming pool, gym and spa, and 114 exclusive residential apartments.

There is also a five-storey viewing gallery called 'The View from the Shard' that is open to the public every day from 9am to 10pm daily except Christmas. To get to 'The View from the Shard', two high-speed lifts take you to the 68th level in just 30 seconds. From there you can make your way to the triple-height glass atrium on Level 69 where you have a 360 degree, 64km incredible vista of London. And for those who want to look up at the 'shards of glass' that form the spire at the top, you can go to the open-air observation deck on Level 72.

shard *scheggia*
ever since *fin dall'inizio*
bold *audace*
sky-reaching *proteso verso il cielo*
spires *guglie*
storey *piano di un edificio*
reaches *raggiunge*
according to *a seconda di*
make up *compongono, formano*
slender *esile, slanciata*
triple-height *altezza di tre piani*

1 What does the phrase 'a boom in the construction of skyscrapers' mean? [lines 1-2]

A It means the building of skyscrapers is slowing down.

B It means there is an increase in building.

C It means many more tall buildings are being built.

D It means no more tall towers are being built.

2 When was the latest skyscraper completed in London?

A In 1710.

B In April 2012.

C In July 2012.

D In 2000.

3 What do Christopher Wren and Renzo Piano have in common?

A They were both born in the 20th century.

B They both designed tall sailing ships.

C They were both born in London.

D They both designed buildings in London.

4 What did Renzo Piano design in London?

A A sailing ship.

B A church.

C A skyscraper.

D A city.

5 Why is The Shard a 'vertical city'?

A Because it is in a city full of skyscrapers.

B Because it is an elongated 87-storey glass pyramid in London.

C Because it combines home, office and recreational spaces in one skyscraper.

D Because it is a very large office building on the River Thames.

6 Which architectural structure is the tallest?

A Big Ben.

B St Paul's Cathedral.

C Nelson's Column.

D BT Tower.

7 How many levels can people go to in The Shard?

A Fifteen.

B Seventy-two.

C Eighty-seven.

D One hundred and fourteen.

8 Which statement about the viewing gallery is correct?

A It is on the fifth floor.

B It closes at 10am.

C It is open every day.

D It isn't open on December 25th.

9 What are 'shards of glass'? [line 30]

A They are glass panels.

B They are glass skyscrapers.

C They are vertical cities.

D They are glass viewing galleries.

10 Where do you think this text comes from?

A A history book about London.

B A guidebook on London.

C An email from Renzo Piano.

D A historical novel about skyscrapers.

Reading Comprehension 16

Date:..

Leggi il testo e scegli la risposta corretta.

Keeping in touch

From: gemma@myemail.gb
To: matt@youremail.gb
Subject: contact

Hi Matt,

Sorry I haven't been in touch sooner, but ever since school started in September, I've been loaded down with homework! I've never had so many assignments, projects and presentations to prepare for school in my life! Maths is my hardest subject this year. My teacher's quite young and rather handsome, but very strict! He gives us a test every week and mountains of homework to do at the weekends! I really believe he thinks we are university students, not high school students! I wish I were back in middle school!

Guess what! I've broken up with Luca... or rather he broke up with me (about three weeks ago). He said that we were too different and he needed space. Well, I was really upset for about a day or two and then I realised that he was right. We really never laughed or had much fun together. Plus, he never paid any attention to me because he was always busy texting his friends or ringing them up. And when he had time for me, he just talked about the latest apps he wanted to download on his mobile or about some stupid football match his school team won! He never once asked me anything about my volleyball team. So now I'm on my own and doing all the things I love to do: going to the cinema, listening to music, shopping, etc, etc!

How are things with your new girlfriend Nicole? She sounded really nice when you described her to me in your last @ - tall, beautiful, blonde, intelligent and from Australia! Are you sure you aren't going out with Nicole Kidman? Ha! Ha! Ha!

Mum told me you were doing really well at university and that you might be home for a long weekend, sometime in early November. I hope you'll be here on the fifth, because Alicia's planning a party to celebrate Guy Fawkes Night. But if you can't make that party, maybe you'll be home for our neighbour's Diwali party. This year the Hindu festival is in November, not October. Remember last year's party! Everything was so spectacular: the food, the house decorations, the music, the candles and, of course, the fireworks!

Take care and don't forget to study! We need a good doctor in the family!

See you in about three weeks! ☺ ☺ ☺

Gemma

loaded down with *sommerso di* **broken up with** *lasciato, rotto*

1 **Why doesn't Gemma write to Matt very often?**
A Because she can't keep in contact.
B Because she has to study a lot.
C Because she is never at home.
D Because she doesn't like Maths.

2 **What school does Gemma go to?**
A The same school Matt does.
B High school.
C Middle school.
D University.

3 **Which statement is NOT true about Gemma's Maths teacher?**
A He teaches university students.
B He is very good looking.
C He gives a lot of homework.
D He isn't a very permissive teacher.

4 **Luca was Gemma's...**
A brother.
B friend.
C boyfriend.
D classmate.

5 **What didn't Luca like doing when he was with Gemma?**
A Talking about football.
B Texting his friends.
C Talking about new apps for his mobile.
D Talking about volleyball.

6 **Some of Gemma's interests are...**
A music, films and clothes.
B football, volleyball and films.
C volleyball, music and shopping.
D texting, music and films.

7 **What does the phrase 'going out with Nicole' mean? [line 22]**
A It means you are visiting Nicole.
B It means you are dating Nicole.
C It means you are going away with Nicole.
D It means you are living with Nicole.

8 **Diwali is a Hindu festival that is...**
A celebrated in October.
B celebrated in November.
C celebrated on 5th November.
D celebrated in October or November.

9 **Who do you think Matt is?**
A Gemma's brother.
B Gemma's neighbour.
C Gemma's classmate.
D Gemma's ex-boyfriend.

10 **When did Gemma write the email to Matt?**
A In September.
B In October.
C In November.
D Three months ago.

Date:...

Leggi il testo e scegli la risposta corretta.

Long distance running and marathons

Run, Pheidippides, run!

A marathon is a 42.195 kilometre road race. Marathon running, also known as long distance running, has become a very popular sport in recent years. The reasons why more people are running long distances today are numerous: to keep fit, to see what they are capable of doing, to have a sense of achievement, or to win a medal in the Olympics. However, long distance running has not always been considered a sport. In ancient civilisations long distance running was a necessity; it served as a means of communication, a way to send important messages from city to city. According to legend, a Greek messenger named Pheidippides ran about forty kilometres non-stop, from the battlefield at Marathon to Athens, to announce that the Greeks had defeated the Persian Army in 490BC. Many centuries later, in 1896, long distance running was finally recognised as a sport, when Pierre de Coubertin and the Olympic Committee for the first modern Olympics in Athens decided to honour Pheidippides' legendary run by including the marathon as an Olympic event.

The Boston Marathon

The first modern Olympic Games provided the inspiration for the Boston Marathon. In fact, it was set up the following year by a group of Olympic athletes from Boston, who had seen the marathon race in Athens. Only eighteen runners entered Boston's first marathon, but the marathon has grown in popularity through the decades and now around 20,000 people run it every year. The Boston Marathon became the first marathon to allow women to compete in 1972, and also the first one to include a wheelchair competition in 1975. It is the oldest annual non-Olympic marathon in the world.

The New York City Marathon

The first New York City Marathon was run in 1970. It was a modest event with only 127 entrants. The 2011 edition holds the record for being the biggest marathon ever held anywhere. There were more than 140,000 applicants, 50,000 entrants, 47,000 finishers, 2.5 million spectators along the course, 350 million television viewers worldwide, and 3,500 runners from Italy, the country with the most participants outside the US. In 2012, for the first time since its inception, the NYC Marathon had to be cancelled because of the violent impact Hurricane Sandy had on the city.

The London Marathon

On 29th March 1981, 7,747 runners participated in the first London Marathon. Since then, almost a million people have crossed its finishing line. The London Marathon is known as the largest fundraising event in the world. More than three quarters of the participants run to raise money for a good cause. It is estimated that more than £500 million have been raised for hundreds of charitable causes by London Marathon runners since 1981.

achievement *realizzazione*
battlefield *campo di battaglia*
applicants *candidati*
inception *inizio*
fundraising *raccolta di fondi*
estimated *stimato*

1 **A marathon is a race that is 42.195 km...**
A far.
B distance.
C long.
D length.

2 **Why did people run long distances thousands of years ago?**
A To keep fit.
B To have a sense of achievement.
C To win gold medals at the Olympics.
D To communicate.

3 **The legend says that Pheidippides...**
A wrote a message to the people of Athens.
B ran 40kms to Marathon.
C ran 40kms without stopping.
D defeated the Persian Army.

4 **When was the first Boston Marathon run?**
A In 1896.
B In 1897.
C In 1972.
D In 1975.

5 **The first Boston Marathon was organised by...**
A a group of 18 marathon runners.
B the Olympic committee.
C some Olympic athletes.
D some businessmen from Boston.

6 **Why was the first NYC Marathon a 'modest event'? [line 46]**
A Because it began 73 years after the Boston Marathon.
B Because there were not many competitors.
C Because there weren't any spectators.
D Because it wasn't shown on TV.

7 **About how many people ran in the 2011 NYC Marathon?**
A Two point five million.
B One hundred and forty thousand.
C Fifty thousand.
D Forty-seven thousand.

8 **Which statement about the NYC Marathon is FALSE?**
A It was not held in 2012.
B You can watch it on TV.
C 3,500 Italians participated in 2011.
D Fewer than 47,000 runners finished the race in 2011.

9 **What does the phrase 'to raise money for a good cause' mean? [lines 67-68]**
A To make money to help someone or something.
B To make money to buy something you want.
C To make money to enter marathons.
D To make money to have a good life.

10 **Where do you think this text comes from?**
A A History book.
B A novel about a marathon runner.
C A travel guidebook.
D A magazine or newspaper.

Date:..

Leggi il testo e scegli la risposta corretta.

Money matters

Money, money, money. You can earn it, you can spend it, you can save it and you can even lose it. But what exactly is it? Money is a medium of exchange which facilitates transactions. The size, shape and form of money have changed considerably throughout history, but it has always been used to buy or sell something.

Before money was invented, people traded their goods and services for the things they needed or wanted. This non-monetary system is called bartering. It is similar to swapping: I'll give you my Bruce Springsteen CD if you give me your black jeans. But bartering is time-consuming and a difficult way to trade as it isn't always possible to establish the value of goods and to find someone who has what you want when you want it.

Then, in the third millennium BC many cultures around the world began using commodities - salt, sheep, shells, precious stones, grains, etc. - as a medium of exchange. This monetary system, called commodity money, facilitated trade because the items used were valued by everyone. However, there were some disadvantages: the commodities used were perishable, difficult to store, heavy to carry around and had to be weighed.

The next form of money was metal money. It was easier to transport and had a fixed standard of value. The Chinese began minting metal coins, which were made of bronze, iron or copper and had holes in the centres so they could be carried on a string, around 1000BC. The first coins to be minted outside China were in Lydia, an ancient country in the area of modern day Turkey, in 640BC, and were made of gold and silver. Metal money was quickly adopted by the ancient Greeks, the Romans and other Mediterranean civilisations.

At the end of the tenth century AD, paper money was invented. The first banknotes were printed in China, and not in Europe, because: 1) the Chinese had learned how to make paper in 105AD, almost a thousand years before the first paper mill in Europe appeared; 2) the Chinese had invented woodblock printing in 220AD and then moveable type printing in 1040AD, more than 400 years before Gutenberg printed the first book in Europe. Paper money permitted the Chinese to buy and sell goods faster and more efficiently as they no longer had to carry around hundreds of heavy strings of coins.

But the spread of paper money in Europe was slow because people preferred gold and silver coins to paper money. When the first printed banknote in Europe was issued by the Swedish Stockholm Bank in 1661, people questioned its value. It was only in the 1800s after European governments adopted the gold standard, guaranteeing the exchange of banknotes for gold, that the use of paper money started gaining acceptance.

Today e-money (electronic money) is rapidly replacing paper and metal money for everyday transactions over the internet. Who knows what form money will have in the future? But whatever form of money is invented, it will, without a doubt, offer people an easier, faster and more convenient way to buy and sell.

medium of exchange *mezzo di scambio*
commodities *materie prime, merci*
perishable *deperibile*
weighed *pesato*
began minting *iniziarono a coniare*
paper mill *cartiera*
woodblock printing *stampa con matrice in legno*
moveable type printing *stampa a caratteri mobili*

1 **Which phrase best completes the sentence? Money is...**
A used to buy things.
B used to sell things.
C not used in transactions.
D a medium of exchange.

2 **What statement about bartering is TRUE?**
A You need lots of money to barter.
B Bartering takes a lot of time.
C It is easy to find people to barter with.
D Bartering was not the first way people traded.

3 **Which is NOT a commodity?**
A Food.
B Fish.
C Sunflower seeds.
D People.

4 **When was commodity money first used?**
A Around 4000-4999 years ago.
B Around 3000-3999 years ago.
C Around 2000-2999 years ago.
D In the year 3000BC.

5 **Why was trading in commodities better than bartering?**
A Because commodities were perishable.
B Because you needed a lot of space for storage.
C Because commodities were easy to transport.
D Because the commodities used were valuable.

6 **Where were the first coins minted outside China?**
A In Rome.
B In Turkey.
C In Lydia.
D In Greece.

7 **The coins minted in 640BC...**
A had to be weighed.
B had a set value.
C had holes in the centres.
D were made of copper.

8 **What did the Chinese NOT do?**
A They made the first banknotes.
B They invented moveable type printing in 1040AD.
C They started using paper money before the Europeans.
D They printed the first book in Europe.

9 **How did paper money change people's lives?**
A It made it easier to buy things on the internet.
B It facilitated transactions.
C More money could be taken abroad.
D They stopped using coins.

10 **Why are new forms of money always being developed?**
A To conduct transactions more efficiently.
B To encourage people to use more money.
C To help people spend less money.
D To guarantee fewer transactions.

Date:...

Leggi il testo e scegli la risposta corretta.

Roald Dahl: On becoming a writer

A fiction writer is a person who invents stories. But how does one start out on a job like this? How does one become a full-time professional fiction writer?

Charles Dickens found it easy. At the age of 24, he simply sat down and wrote *The Pickwick Papers*, which became an immediate best-seller. But Dickens was a genius, and geniuses are different from the rest of us.

In this century (it was not always so in the last one), just about every single writer who has finally become successful in the world of fiction has started out in some other job- a schoolteacher, perhaps, or a doctor or a journalist or a lawyer. The first attempts at writing have therefore always had to be done in spare time, usually at night.

The reason for this is obvious. When you are grown-up, it is necessary to earn a living. To earn a living, you must get a job. You must, if possible, get a job that guarantees you so much money a week. But however much you may want to take up fiction writing as a career, it would be pointless to go along to a publisher and say, 'I want a job as a fiction writer.' If you did that, he would tell you to buzz off and write the book first. And even if you brought a finished book to him and he liked it well enough to publish it, he still wouldn't give you a job. He would give you an advance of perhaps one or two thousand dollars, which he would get back again later by deducting it from your royalties. (A royalty, by the way, is the money that a writer gets from the publisher for each copy of his book that is sold. The average royalty a writer gets is 10% of the price of the book itself in the bookshop. Thus for a book selling at 7 dollars, the writer would get seventy cents.)

It is very common for a hopeful fiction writer to spend two years of his spare time writing a book which no publisher will publish. For that he gets nothing at all except a sense of frustration.

If he is fortunate enough to have a book accepted by a publisher, the odds are that as a first novel it will sell only about three thousand copies. That will earn him about twenty-one hundred dollars. Most novels take at least one year to write, and twenty-one hundred dollars a year is not enough to live on these days. So you can see why a budding fiction writer invariably has to start out in another job first of all. If he doesn't, he will almost certainly starve.

lawyer *avvocato*
attempts *tentativi*
earn *guadagnare*
pointless *inutile*
buzz off *andarsene*
an advance *un anticipo (di denaro)*
royalties *diritti d'autore*
the odds *le probabilità*
budding *in erba*
starve *morire di fame*

1 **According to the text, what do fiction writers do?**
A They make inventions.
B They make up stories.
C They write non-fiction books.
D They look for full time jobs.

2 **'*The Pickwick Papers*', by Charles Dickens, ...**
A was a very expensive book.
B was an easy book to read.
C was a very successful book.
D did not sell very well.

3 **Last century most writers...**
A started writing when they were 24.
B wrote books in their spare time.
C never had second jobs.
D were school teachers.

4 **When do first time fiction writers usually write?**
A In the morning.
B When they are at their jobs.
C When they are not working.
D At the weekends.

5 **What does 'to earn a living' mean? [line 11]**
A It means to have two jobs.
B It means to make money in your spare time.
C It means to be successful at your job.
D It means to make money to be able to live.

6 **What is NOT true about publishers?**
A They always publish writers' books.
B They give advances to writers.
C They pay royalties to writers.
D They publish all types of books.

7 **Why do many prospective writers get frustrated?**
A Because they aren't working.
B Because they haven't any money.
C Because no one will publish their works.
D Because they spend too much time writing.

8 **How much would a writer be paid in royalties if 100 books were sold at a price of €10 per book?**
A €1
B €10
C €100
D €1,000

9 **If you want to become a full-time writer, you should have another job...**
A so that you can write in your spare time.
B because you will need some money to live on.
C so that you will be able to find a publisher.
D because you will not finish your book.

10 **Why do you think the writer wrote the text?**
A To discourage people from becoming fiction writers.
B To give advice to promising fiction writers.
C To inform writers about publishers.
D To encourage people to write fiction.

Date:..

1

You will hear five short conversations.
You will hear each conversation twice.
There is one question for each conversation.
For questions 1 – 5, put a tick (✓) on the right answer.

Example:

How many people were at the cinema?

A	B	C
5	15	50
A	B	C ✓

1 What is the weather like?

A

B

C

2 Where is Tom going for his holiday this year?

A	B	C
Ireland	France	Scotland

Date:..

3 What time was Sam's appointment?

A

B

C

4 How far is the nearest garage?

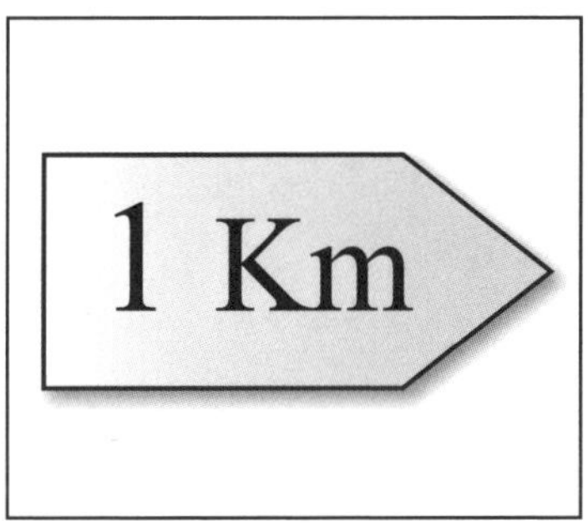

A

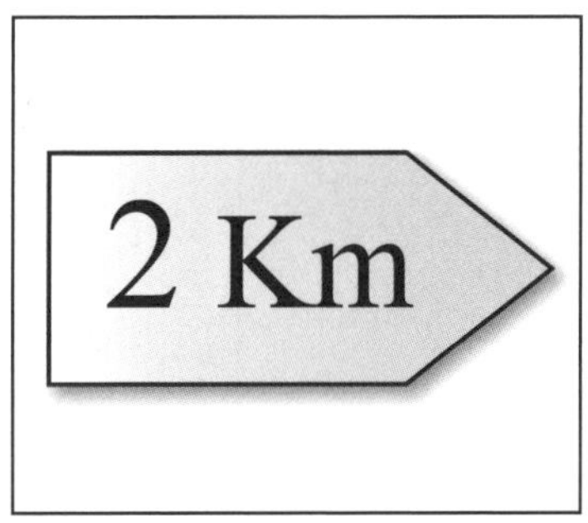

B

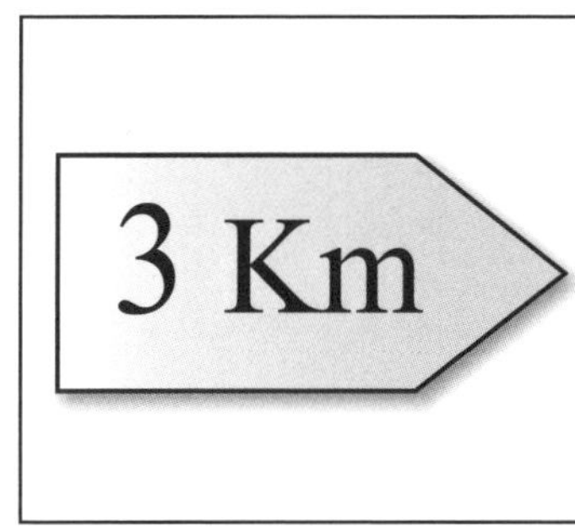

C

5 Which pet does Mrs. Jones like?

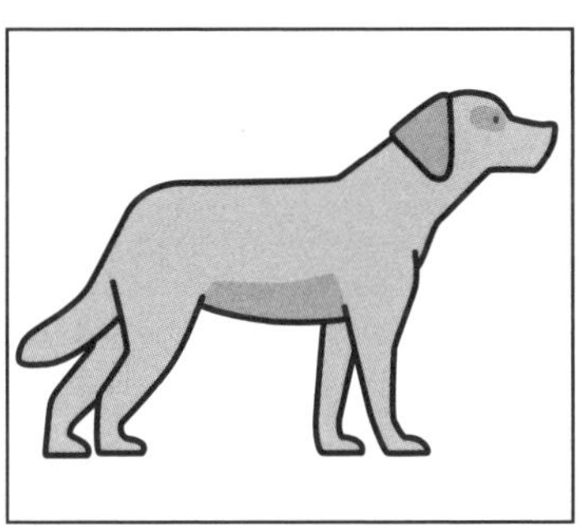

A

B

C

Date:...

2

Listen to Jake talking to a friend about the weekend.
What did each person do?
For questions 1 – 5, write a letter (A – H) next to each person.
You will hear the conversation twice.

Example:

Sam [A]

---

1 Fred [ ]

2 Dennis [ ]

3 Clare [ ]

4 Jake [ ]

5 Sue [ ]

A went camping
B went camping with Sam
C went babysitting
D went bowling
E played golf
F visited a friend in hospital
G visited her grandma
H broke a leg

Date:..

3 🔊

Listen to Sue talking to a friend about her holiday in Europe.
What did she do in each place?
For questions 6 – 10, write a letter (A – H) next to each country.
You will hear the conversation twice.

Example:

Belgium [B]

---

6 France [ ]

7 Luxembourg [ ]

8 Italy [ ]

9 Switzerland [ ]

10 Holland [ ]

A saw lots of tulips

B visited a boat museum

C had a city tour

D went up a famous tower

E walked in the mountains

F had excellent food

G lost her passport

H visited a beautiful palace

Date:..

4

Listen to Sarah talking about her school.
For questions 1 – 5, tick A, B or C.
You will hear the conversation twice.

Example:

Where does Sarah go?

- [x] A Chantry Secondary
- B Chantry Primary
- C Chantry Junior

1 How many pupils are there?

- A about 2000 pupils
- B about 1200 pupils
- C about 1300 pupils

2 Where is the playing field?

- A near the gym
- B behind the running track
- C behind the gym

3 She can go swimming

- A in winter
- B in summer
- C all year

4 P.E. lessons are on

- A Tuesday afternoons
- B Thursday afternoons
- C Wednesday afternoons

5 What do they do when it rains?

- A do gym
- B play hockey
- C play tennis

Date:...

5

Listen to Matthew talking to Jane about Christmas shopping.
For questions 1 – 5, tick A, B or C.
You will hear the conversation twice.

Example:

What did Matthew buy?

- [x] A a vase
- B a book
- C a tie

---

1 What does Matthew want to buy for his sister?

- A some Lego
- B a book
- C a vase

2 Matthew's brother is

- A good with his hands
- B good at taking photographs
- C good at reading

3 What does his sister love?

- A reading
- B taking photos
- C travelling

4 The book about Rome is

- A in the bookshop
- B on the map
- C in the bag

5 What does Jane's dad want?

- A some chocolate
- B a tie
- C some photographs

Date:..

6

You will hear a man asking for information about a theatre.
Listen and complete questions 1 – 5.
You will hear the conversation twice.

THEATRE		
Theatre		The Rainbow
Title of play	1	The Pirate ....
Day of performance	2	....
Tickets cost	3	£ .... for adults,
	4	£ .... for children.
Performance starts at	5	....

Date:..

7

You will hear some information about a castle.
Listen and complete the notes 1 – 5.
You will hear the information twice.

HEMINGSTONE CASTLE

YOU CAN SEE

Downstairs:

Entrance Hall		old medieval map
Hemingstone family crest	1	a white .... with 3 crowns
Dining Hall	2	long wooden .... and chairs
Upstairs:		
Left	3	exhibition of beautiful old ....
Right	4	the first Duke's original ....
Price of guidebook	5	£ ....

Date:...

1 **Completa la domanda.**
... are you from?
A What
B Where
C Who
D When

2 **Completa la frase.**
They are from New York. ... American.
A There
B They're
C Their
D There are

3 **Scegli la frase corretta.**
A There isn't no water in the fridge.
B There is any water in the fridge.
C There is some water in the fridge.
D There isn't some water in the fridge.

4 **Completa la conversazione.**
How old are you?
A I'm fine, thanks.
B I'm thirteen.
C I have thirteen.
D I'm tired.

5 **Scegli la domanda per questa risposta.**
It's sunny and hot today!
A How are you?
B Is it rainy?
C What's the weather like?
D What's like the weather?

6 **Completa la domanda.**
We're going to the cinema this evening.
... with us?
A Are you coming
B Are you come
C Did you come
D Come you

7 **Completa la frase.**
She ... home when the storm began.
A walked
B was walking
C is walking
D walks

8 **Completa la frase.**
My sister goes to the fitness centre;
she's very ... !
A lazy
B selfish
C energetic
D boring

9 **Quale frase esprime *abilità/capacità*?**
A I have to play tennis.
B I must play tennis.
C I can play tennis.
D I may play tennis.

10 **In quale frase è usato il *pronome personale complemento*?**
A I like Marta.
B I like her.
C I like Marta and her friends.
D I like hers.

Date:..

1 Scegli la domanda per questa risposta.
I'm going to play tennis tomorrow.
A What do you do?
B Where are you going tomorrow?
C What are you going to do tomorrow?
D What do you doing tomorrow?

2 Completa la domanda.
... they arrive on time? No, they were late!
A Do
B Did
C Will
D Can

3 Scegli la frase corretta.
A Monica Bellucci is the famousest actress in the world.
B Monica Bellucci is the more famous actress in the world.
C Monica Bellucci is the most famous actress in the world.
D Monica Bellucci is the famouser actress in the world.

4 Scegli la trasformazione corretta della frase nel discorso indiretto.
'I'll call you later!'
A He said he calls me later.
B He said he would call me later.
C He said he called me later.
D He said I would call him later.

5 Quale frase NON è corretta?
A He will fly to Paris next week, won't he?
B He won't fly to Paris next week, will he?
C He's been to Paris, hasn't he?
D He's been to Paris, isn't he?

6 Completa la conversazione.
Can I borrow your mobile, please?
A Sorry, but I'm using it!
B Sorry, but I used it!
C Sorry, but I've used it!
D Sorry, but I'm not using it!

7 Completa la frase.
If I ... you, I ... stay up late.
A am / will
B will / would
C were / wouldn't
D was / will

8 Completa con la parola appropriata.
Janet won the lottery, she was so ... !
A angry
B lucky
C sad
D boring

9 Quale frase esprime un *invito*?
A Would you like to go for a pizza?
B Would you like a pizza?
C Do you like pizza?
D Will you like a pizza?

10 In quale frase *like* è usato come verbo?
A What's he like?
B Andrea likes sports.
C He looks like his mother.
D He plays volleyball like a champion!

Date:..

1 **Completa la domanda.**
Where ... last night?
A went you
B did you go
C are you went
D did you went

2 **Completa la frase.**
Alex and Timmy always chat with ... friends on Facebook.
A there
B they're
C their
D theirs

3 **Scegli la frase corretta.**
A When does he usually do his homework?
B When does he usually his homework?
C When he usually does his homework?
D When does he do usually his homework?

4 **Completa la conversazione.**
How did you get to Milan?
A In train.
B By train.
C With the train.
D On the train.

5 **Scegli la domanda per questa risposta.**
That's a good idea!
A Would you like to go out for a pizza tonight?
B Do you like pizza?
C Did you go out for a pizza?
D Have you had some pizza yet?

6 **Scegli la frase corretta.**
A I'm younger that my brother.
B I'm younger then my brother.
C I'm younger than my brother.
D I'm younger of my brother.

7 **Quale frase NON è corretta?**
A The team's new goalkeeper plays very well.
B The team's new goalkeeper plays much better than Peter does.
C The team's new goalkeeper plays well.
D The team's new goalkeeper plays very better.

8 **Completa con la parola appropriata.**
Timmy never lends his mp3 player to any of his friends. He's a really ... kid.
A generous
B selfish
C polite
D kind

9 **Scegli quale intenzione comunicativa esprime la frase seguente.**
I met Barbara at the party yesterday.
A Making plans.
B Talking about a past event.
C Introducing people.
D Talking about the weather.

10 **In quale frase *'s* è la forma contratta del verbo essere?**
A Your father's friend's got a new car.
B Your father's car is at the mechanic's.
C Your father's friend's car's got a flat tyre.
D Your father's friend's new car's fantastic.

1 Completa la frase.
If you want to be healthy, ... junk food.
A don't eat
B eat
C let's eat
D you can eat

2 Completa la domanda.
Will you go out if it ... ?
A will rain
B rains
C it was raining
D rained

3 Scegli la trasformazione corretta della frase nel discorso indiretto.
'What time does she want to go?'
A He asked me what time she will go.
B He asked me what time she wants to go.
C He asked me what time she went.
D He asked me what time she wanted to go.

4 Scegli la frase corretta.
A Have ever you been to China?
B Have you ever been to China?
C Have you been never to China?
D Have you been ever to China?

5 Completa la conversazione.
How long are you going to be in NYC?
A Two weeks ago.
B About two weeks.
C For the last two weeks.
D In two weeks.

6 Scegli la frase corretta.
A She can coming to Rome next weekend.
B She cans come to Rome next weekend.
C She could to come to Rome next weekend.
D She might come to Rome next weekend.

7 Scegli la frase che ha lo stesso significato della seguente.
My father is as old as my mother.
A My mother is younger than my father.
B My father is older than my mother.
C My parents are both the same age.
D My father isn't as young as my mother.

8 Completa con la parola appropriata.
They ... a lot of new friends on holiday last year!
A meet
B meat
C met
D mat

9 Quale frase esprime una *proposta*?
A Why don't we go to the cinema?
B Why will you go to the cinema?
C Why didn't you go to the cinema?
D Why are you going to the cinema?

10 In quale frase il *present continuous* è usato come futuro?
A My brother is working in London for a few months.
B My brother is working in London next month.
C My brother is working in London at present.
D My brother is always working in London.

Date:..

1 **Quale frase NON è corretta?**
A I moved to New York five years ago.
B I have lived in New York for five years.
C I will move to New York next year.
D I lived in New York since five years.

2 **Completa la frase.**
I'm sorry I can't come ... your party!
A at
B to
C too
D two

3 **Scegli la frase corretta.**
A What weather is like?
B How the weather is?
C What's the weather like?
D What's like the weather?

4 **Completa la risposta.**
Did you like the film? Yes, I ... .
A liked
B did like
C did it
D did

5 **Completa la conversazione.**
Which T-shirt do you prefer?
A It's too small.
B The red one!
C Not much!
D Very much!

6 **Scegli la domanda per questa risposta.**
I go to the pool twice a week.
A Have you been swimming?
B How often do you go swimming?
C How much do you go swimming?
D Did you go swimming?

7 **Scegli la frase che ha lo stesso significato della seguente.**
A motorbike is cheaper than a car.
A A motorbike doesn't cost as much as a car.
B A car isn't as expensive as a motorbike.
C A motorbike is as expensive as a car.
D A motorbike is more expensive than a car.

8 **Completa con la parola appropriata.**
What do you usually do in summer?
I go to the ... .
A house
B see
C seas
D seaside

9 **Quale frase esprime una *richiesta*?**
A Could you help me with my homework, please?
B Can I help you with my homework?
C Shall I help you with my homework?
D Should you help me with my homework?

10 **In quale frase *that* è usato come aggettivo dimostrativo?**
A Who's that boy over there?
B That was a very exciting match!
C This is the car that Peter bought last week.
D He told me that he was coming home late.

1 Scegli la frase corretta.

A I never have lunch at school.
B I have never lunch at school.
C I don't never have lunch at school.
D I don't have never lunch at school.

2 Completa la frase.

I've got a new smartphone. I've had it ... .

A two days ago
B since two days
C in two days
D for two days

3 Quale frase NON è corretta?

A I'm so hungry. I'll have a snack!
B I'm so hungry. I'm having a snack!
C I'm so hungry. I'm going to have a snack!
D I'm so hungry. I had a snack.

4 Completa la conversazione.

We're having a party this evening.
Will you bring some CDs, please?

A I'll bring.
B Yes, I am.
C Sure!
D I would.

5 Scegli la frase che ha lo stesso significato della seguente.

Giorgio is the youngest student in the class.

A Someone is younger than Giorgio in the class.
B Giorgio is as young as the other students in the class.
C Nobody is younger than Giorgio in the class.
D Giorgio is older than the other students in the class.

6 Scegli la domanda per questa risposta.

Yes, I've been there many times!

A Are you going to London?
B Have you ever visited London?
C Did you go to London?
D Have you gone to London?

7 Scegli la frase corretta.

A Mum can't find her sunglasses nowhere.
B Mum can't find her sunglasses somewhere.
C Mum can't find her sunglasses anywhere.
D Mum can't find her glasses everywhere.

8 Completa con la parola appropriata.

Judy spends hours chatting with her friend. She is a very ... girl.

A rude
B shy
C moody
D talkative

9 Quale frase esprime un *obbligo*?

A You must stop when the traffic light is red!
B You should stop when the traffic light is red!
C You can't stop when the traffic light is red!
D You can stop when the traffic light is red!

10 In quale frase *light* è usato come verbo?

A The British usually have a light lunch.
B Save electricity! Switch the light off, please!
C Let's light the candles on the birthday cake!
D My favourite colour is light blue.

Date:..

1 **Completa la frase.**
She ... invite Brad to her party if she ... his mobile number!
A would / has
B will / had
C would / had
D would / will have

2 **Scegli la frase corretta.**
A We had to wait half an hour to get the tickets.
B We must to wait half an hour to get the tickets.
C We could to wait half an hour to get the tickets.
D We might to wait half an hour to get the tickets.

3 **Scegli la trasformazione corretta della frase in forma passiva.**
Shakespeare wrote a lot of plays.
A A lot of plays written by Shakespeare.
B A lot of plays are written by Shakespeare.
C A lot of plays were written by Shakespeare.
D A lot of plays wrote by Shakespeare.

4 **Quale frase NON è corretta?**
A I haven't seen him since last week.
B I haven't seen him for last week.
C I didn't see him last week.
D I haven't seen him for a long time.

5 **Scegli la trasformazione corretta della frase nel discorso indiretto.**
'I'm going to buy a new tablet.'
A She said she buys a new tablet.
B She said she will buy a new tablet.
C She said she went to buy a new tablet.
D She said she was going to buy a new tablet.

6 **Completa la conversazione.**
When can I come and visit you?
A Not at all!
B Whenever you want!
C Yes, please!
D No, thanks!

7 **Scegli la frase che ha lo stesso significato della seguente.**
My father works in a bank; he started working there twenty years ago.
A My father still works in the same bank after twenty years.
B My father worked in the same bank for twenty years.
C My father doesn't work in the same bank after twenty years.
D My father hasn't worked in the same bank for twenty years.

8 **Completa con la parola appropriata.**
Passengers have to ... an hour before their flight takes off.
A check up
B check in
C check out
D check

9 **Scegli quale intenzione comunicativa esprime la frase seguente.**
What do you think of Coldplay's new song?
A Making plans.
B Talking about a past event.
C Introducing people.
D Asking for an opinion.

10 **In quale frase *fair* è usato come sostantivo?**
A We went to the fun fair and had hotdogs.
B She's got fair hair and dark eyes.
C Fair play is very important in sport!
D It isn't fair cheating at exams!

1 Scegli la frase corretta.

A You won't pass the exam if you don't study harder.

B You won't pass the exam if you won't study harder.

C You won't pass the exam if you didn't study harder.

D You won't pass the exam if you wouldn't study harder.

2 Scegli la domanda per questa risposta.

Yes, please! I haven't eaten since breakfast!

A Have you got a tuna sandwich?

B What about having a tuna sandwich?

C Did you have a sandwich?

D Do you like a sandwich?

3 Scegli la trasformazione corretta della frase nel discorso indiretto.

'Don't forget my birthday!'

A She said me not to forget her birthday.

B She told me not to forget her birthday.

C She told me to forget not her birthday.

D She told me to not forget my birthday.

4 Completa la frase.

Pat ... me while I ... TV.

A rings / watched

B rang / am watching

C rang / was watching

D rang / watched

5 Completa la conversazione.

Linda doesn't speak German.

A David doesn't, too.

B Neither David does.

C David doesn't neither.

D Neither does David.

6 Scegli la frase corretta.

A My uncle which lives in Dublin is visiting us next week.

B My uncle who lives in Dublin is visiting us next week.

C My uncle he lives in Dublin is visiting us next week.

D My uncle who he lives in Dublin is visiting us next week.

7 Scegli la frase corretta nella forma passiva.

They serve breakfast from 7.00 to 8.30.

A Breakfast is serve from 7.00 to 8.30.

B Breakfast was served from 7.00 to 8.30.

C Breakfast has served from 7.00 to 8.30.

D Breakfast is served from 7.00 to 8.30.

8 Completa con la parola appropriata.

When you ... the bus, walk as far as the bank and take the second left.

A get up

B get on

C get off

D get out

9 Quale frase esprime una *decisone immediata*?

A It's sunny and hot! I'll go for a swim.

B It's sunny and hot! I should go for a swim.

C It's sunny and hot! I may go for a swim.

D It's sunny and hot! I might go for a swim.

10 In quale frase *where* è usato come pronome relativo?

A Where were you born?

B This is the house where I used to live.

C I don't know where they are from.

D I don't remember where I left my keys!

Date:..

1 **Quale frase NON è corretta?**
A That is the best book for to learn English.
B That is the best book to learn English.
C If you want to learn English, that's the best book.
D That is the best book for English learners.

2 **Completa la conversazione.**
How often do you surf the Net?
A On Saturday.
B Next Saturday.
C Every day.
D At the moment.

3 **Scegli la trasformazione corretta della frase in discorso diretto.**
She asked me what I was watching on TV.
A 'What did you watch on TV?'
B 'What are you watching on TV?'
C 'What do you watch on TV?'
D 'What are you going to watch on TV?'

4 **Completa la frase.**
We've known each other ... 2010.
A for
B since
C from
D in

5 **Scegli la frase corretta.**
A She is the lady the handbag was stolen.
B She is the lady the handbag of which was stolen.
C She is the lady which the handbag was stolen.
D She is the lady whose handbag was stolen.

6 **Scegli la frase corretta.**
A If I could, I will travel around the world.
B If I can, I would travel around the world.
C If I may, I would travel around the world.
D If I could, I would travel around the world.

7 **Scegli la trasformazione corretta della frase in forma passiva.**
Who created Facebook?
A Who is Facebook created by?
B Who was Facebook created by?
C Who has Facebook created by?
D Who has Facebook been created by?

8 **Completa con la parola appropriata.**
He ... his skateboard and broke his arm.
A fell to
B fell in
C fell off
D fell into

9 **Quale frase esprime un'*offerta*?**
A Would you like some ice cream?
B Do you like some ice cream?
C Let's have some ice cream!
D Can you have some ice cream?

10 **In quale frase *front* è usato come sostantivo?**
A The bus stop is in front of the cinema.
B The front door was left open after the robbery.
C The front of the house has just been repainted.
D The new hotel fronts the ocean.

1 **Completa la frase.**
The British Museum is so amazing!
You ... visit it!
A will
B should
C shall
D mustn't

2 **Scegli la trasformazione corretta della frase in forma passiva.**
They won't open a new library in town.
A A new library isn't opened in town.
B A new library will open in town.
C A new library won't be opened in town.
D A new library isn't being opened in town.

3 **Completa la domanda.**
... mobile is this? Is it yours?
A Who's
B Who
C What
D Whose

4 **Scegli la trasformazione corretta della frase in discorso diretto.**
She said she didn't need to take a taxi, she could walk there.
A 'I don't need to take a taxi, I can walk there.'
B 'I don't need to take a taxi, I could walk there.'
C 'I didn't need to take a taxi, I can walk there.'
D 'I won't need to take a taxi, I can walk there.'

5 **Completa la conversazione.**
I've lost my keys!
A How much are they?
B Did you buy them?
C Have you looked for them?
D Of course!

6 **Scegli la domanda per questa risposta.**
On January 25th.
A Where were you born?
B How old are you?
C What's the date today?
D When is your birthday?

7 **Scegli la frase che ha lo stesso significato della seguente.**
First we did our homework, then we went to the cinema.
A We went to the cinema, but after that we did our homework.
B We went to the cinema, but before that we did our homework.
C We went to the cinema and after that we did our homework.
D First we went to the cinema and then we did our homework.

8 **Completa con la parola appropriata.**
Yesterday the ... was awesome. It was sunny all day!
A time
B whether
C weather
D waiter

9 **Quale frase esprime una *preferenza*?**
A Could I have some coffee?
B I like coffee.
C I'd rather have some coffee.
D I will have some coffee.

10 **In quale frase *reading* è usato come sostantivo?**
A Reading is my favourite hobby!
B Mum has just bought a nice reading lamp.
C Judy is reading in her bedroom.
D I need a new pair of reading glasses.

Date:...

1 **Scegli la domanda per questa risposta.**
I have lived in Italy for 10 years!
A How much for have you lived in Italy?
B How often have you lived in Italy?
C How long have you lived in Italy?
D How far have you lived in Italy?

2 **Completa la conversazione.**
What are you doing this evening?
A Yes, please!
B Nothing special!
C No, thanks!
D Good idea!

3 **Completa la domanda.**
... is it from London to Manchester?
A How much
B How long
C How far
D How many

4 **Scegli la risposta appropriata.**
What's the matter with you?
A I've got a sore throat.
B I've got a throat.
C I am a sore throat.
D I've got a throat sore.

5 **Scegli la frase corretta.**
A I never have lunch at school.
B I have never lunch at school.
C I don't never have lunch at school.
D I don't have ever lunch at school.

6 **Completa la frase.**
Living in a foreign country is the best way to learn ... the culture and traditions.
A of
B on
C about
D with

7 **Scegli la frase che ha lo stesso significato della seguente.**
Doing sport is more exciting than watching it on TV.
A Doing sport is as exciting as watching it on TV.
B Watching sport on TV is more exciting than doing it.
C Doing sport isn't as exciting as watching it on TV.
D Watching sport on TV is less exciting than doing it.

8 **Completa con la parola appropriata.**
What's his ... ?
He's a cook in a sushi restaurant.
A work
B job
C place
D home

9 **Quale frase esprime un *consiglio*?**
I'm so tired!
A You should go to bed!
B You have to go to bed!
C You must go to bed!
D You may go to bed!

10 **In quale frase *fast* è avverbio?**
A My brother is a fast runner.
B My brother runs fast.
C Planes are faster than cars.
D Fast food is not healthy!

Date:..

1 **Scegli la frase che ha lo stesso significato.**
The last time I heard from Mark was on Sunday.
A I haven't heard from Mark since Sunday.
B I don't hear from Mark since on Sunday.
C I didn't hear from Mark since on Sunday.
D I hear from Mark on Sundays.

2 **Quale frase NON è corretta?**
A While dad was cutting the grass, the lawn mower broke.
B Dad cut the grass when the lawn mower broke.
C Dad was cutting the grass when the lawn mower broke.
D The lawn mower broke while dad was cutting the grass.

3 **Scegli la trasformazione corretta della frase in forma passiva.**
Picasso painted Guernica.
A Guernica is painted by Picasso
B Guernica will be painted by Picasso.
C Guernica was painted by Picasso
D Guernica has been painted by Picasso.

4 **Completa la conversazione.**
I love windsurfing!
A Neither do I.
B So do I.
C But I do.
D Also for me.

5 **Scegli la frase corretta.**
A She had a car accident because she wasn't paying attention.
B She will have a car accident because she wasn't paying attention.
C She has a car accident because she wasn't paying attention.
D She won't have a car accident because she isn't paying attention.

6 **Scegli la domanda per questa risposta.**
8.00
A How far is it?
B How much is it?
C How old is he?
D What's the time?

7 **Completa la frase.**
They were ill, so they ... to the concert.
A weren't going
B didn't go
C aren't going
D don't go

8 **Completa con la parola appropriata.**
We had a lot of ... at the party.
A funny
B fan
C fun
D fine

9 **Quale frase esprime la funzione comunicativa di *offrirsi di fare qualcosa*?**
A Shall I close the door?
B Can I close the door?
C Must I close the door?
D Do I have to close the door?

10 **In quale frase *that* è usato come pronome relativo soggetto?**
A Who's that girl over there?
B That's the student that I told you about!
C That's a very clever dog!
D He is the boy that won the music contest.

Date:..

1 **Scegli la domanda per questa risposta.**
Two years ago.
A Did you go to England?
B When did you go to England?
C How long have you been in England?
D Are you going to England?

2 **Scegli la frase che ha lo stesso significato della seguente.**
They didn't arrive in time to see the concert.
A They were late but they could see the concert.
B They were on time to see the concert.
C They were too early to see the concert.
D They missed the concert because they were late.

3 **Scegli la trasformazione corretta della frase nel discorso indiretto.**
"Why are you so nervous?"
A She wanted to know why I was so nervous.
B She wanted to know because I was so nervous.
C She wanted to know if I was so nervous.
D She wanted to know why I am so nervous.

4 **Quale frase NON è corretta?**
A Shall we meet us at 4pm?
B Let's meet at 4pm?
C Shall we meet at 4pm?
D How about meeting at 4pm?

5 **Completa la conversazione.**
Your hair looks so clean and shiny!
A I've already washed it!
B I've just washed it!
C I've washed it yet!
D I've still washed it!

6 **Completa la frase.**
I'm a bit hungry. I'd like ... to eat.
A nothing
B anyone
C something
D anything

7 **Scegli la frase corretta.**
A He's been nice to you, was he?
B He's been nice to you, hasn't he?
C He's been nice to you, has he?
D He's been nice to you, isn't he?

8. **Completa con la parola appropriata.**
To store files in a computer, click on ... .
A paste
B cut and paste
C print
D save

9 **Quale frase esprime un *divieto*?**
A You needn't cheat during the exam!
B You couldn't cheat during the exam!
C You don't have to cheat during the exam!
D You mustn't cheat during the exam!

10 **In quale frase *set* è usato come aggettivo?**
A We bought a new TV set.
B The actors are working on the set.
C They arrived at the set time.
D I always set the alarm clock before going to bed.

1 Completa la frase.
Don't forget ... me an email when you arrive!
A to sending
B to send
C send
D of sending

2 Scegli la domanda per questa risposta.
Yes, I finished it yesterday!
A Have you finished your project yet?
B Have you finished your project just?
C Have you yet finished your project?
D Have you finished your project already?

3 Completa la conversazione.
What do you think of Adele's latest song?
A I think so!
B I hope so!
C I love it!
D I do!

4 Scegli la trasformazione corretta della frase in forma passiva.
The mechanic has repaired dad's car.
A Dad's car is being repaired.
B Dad's car was repaired.
C Dad's car has been repaired.
D Dad's car had been repaired.

5 Scegli la trasformazione corretta della frase nel discorso indiretto.
'Can I book a room for two nights?'
A She asked if she can book a room for two nights.
B She asked if she could book a room for two nights.
C She asked if she could to book a room for two nights.
D She asked if she booked a room for two nights.

6 Scegli la frase corretta.
A Giulia is much pretty than Anna.
B Giulia is much prettier than Anna.
C Giulia is much more pretty than Anna.
D Giulia is very pretty than Anna.

7 Scegli la frase che ha lo stesso significato della seguente.
Someone will pick you up on your arrival at the airport.
A Someone will arrive at the airport.
B There won't be anyone to pick you up at the airport.
C You will pick someone up at the airport.
D When you arrive someone will be there to pick you up.

8 Completa con la parola appropriata.
The cost of ... is getting higher and higher.
A leave
B living
C live
D life

9 Scegli quale intenzione comunicativa esprime la frase seguente.
Can you tell me how to get to the bank, please?
A Asking for an opinion.
B Making plans.
C Asking for permission.
D Asking the way.

10 In quale frase *one* è usato come pronome?
A My desk is the one near the window.
B They came in one by one.
C The show finished before one.
D I've got one new coin in my collection.

Glossary

Abbreviations

adj.	adjective	aggettivo
adv.	adverb	avverbio
conj.	conjunction	congiunzione
n.	noun	sostantivo
prep.	preposition	preposizione
v.	verb	verbo

A

according to /ə'kɔːdɪŋ tuː/ *prep.* a seconda di
achievement /ə'tʃiːv.mənt/ *n.* realizzazione
advance /əd'vɑːns/ *n.* anticipo (di denaro)
ahead /ə'hed/ *adv.* in anticipo
allow /ə'laʊ/ *v.* concedere
applicant /'æplɪkənt/ *n.* candidato
attempt /ə'tempt/ *n.* tentativo
average /'ævərɪdʒ/ *adj.* medio

B

balance /'bæləns/ *v.* bilanciare
battlefield /'bætlfiːld/ *n.* campo di battaglia
become aware of /bɪ'kʌm ə'weər əv/ *v.* rendersi conto di
blame for /bleɪm fɔːr/ *v.* essere responsabile di
bleaching /'bliːtʃɪŋ/ *n.* sbiancamento
bold /bəʊld/ *adj.* audace
break up with /'breɪk ʌp wɪð/ *v.* rompere (un rapporto)
budding /'bʌdɪŋ/ *adj.* in erba
burst out laughing /bɜːst aʊt 'lɑːfɪŋ/ *v.* scoppiare a ridere
buzz off /bʌz ɒf/ *v.* andarsene

C

caw /kɔː/ *v.* gracchiare
challenge /'tʃælɪndʒ/ *n.* sfida
copper /'kɒpər/ *n.* rame
comeback /'kʌmbæk/ *n.* ritorno
commitment /kə'mɪtmənt/ *n.* impegno
commodity /kə'mɒdətɪ/ *n.* materia prima, merce
commute /kə'mjuːt/ *v.* fare la spola
crown-of-thorns /kraʊn ɒv θɔːnz/ *n.* corona di spine
crow /krəʊ/ *n.* cornacchia
cut down on /kʌt daʊn ɒn/ *v.* ridurre
cut off /kʌt ɒf/ *v.* tagliare

D

drive towards /draɪv tə'wɔːdz/ *v.* condurre a

E

earn /ɜːn/ *v.* guadagnare
estimate /'estɪmət/ *v.* stimare, valutare
ever since /'evər sɪns/ *adv.* fin dall'inizio
expectation /ˌekspek'teɪʃn/ *n.* aspettativa

F

fight off /faɪt ɒf/ *v.* combattere
fundraising /'fʌndreɪzɪŋ/ *n.* raccolta di fondi

G

goods /gʊdz/ *n.* merce
grab /græb/ *v.* afferrare
grumble /'grʌmbl/ *v.* brontolare

H

halve /hɑːv/ *v.* dimezzare
hare /heər/ *n.* lepre
have a crush on /hæv ə krʌʃ ɒn/ *v.* avere una cotta per
heal /hiːl/ *v.* guarire
heating /'hiːtɪŋ/ *n.* riscaldamento
hedgehog /'hedʒhɒg/ *n.* riccio
heritage /'herɪtɪdʒ/ *n.* radici, legami familiari

I

ice sheet /aɪs ʃiːt/ *n.* lastra di ghiaccio
inception /ɪn'sepʃn/ *n.* inizio
intake /'ɪnteɪk/ *n.* assunzione
IU /aɪjuː/ *n.* UI (0.025 microgrammi)

L

lame /leɪm/ *adj.* zoppo
land /lænd/ *v.* atterrare
lawn /lɔːn/ *n.* prato
lawyer /'lɔːjər/ *n.* avvocato
load down with /ləʊd daʊn wɪð/ *v.* sovraccaricare di

M

mackerel /'mæk.rəl/ *n.* sgombro
make up /meɪk ʌp/ *v.* comporre, inventare (una storia)
make fun of /meɪk fʌn ɒv/ *v.* prendere in giro
mark out /mɑːk aʊt/ *v.* delimitare
medium of exchange /'miːdɪəm ɒv ɪks'tʃeɪndʒ/ *n.* mezzo di scambio
meet /miːt/ *v.* soddisfare
mint /mɪnt/ *v.* coniare
moveable type printing /'muː.və.bl taɪp 'prɪn.tɪŋ/ *n.* stampa a caratteri mobili

N

nod /nɒd/ *v.* fare cenno

O

odds /ɒdz/ *n.* probabilità
out sold /aʊt səʊld/ *v.* superato nelle vendite
ownership /'əʊ.nə.ʃɪp/ *n.* proprietà

P

pantry /'pæn.tri/ *n.* dispensa
paper mill /'peɪpər mɪl/ *n.* cartiera
peak /piːk/ *adj.* di massima importanza
perishable /'perɪʃəbl/ *adj.* deperibile
pointless /'pɔɪntlɪs/ *adj.* inutile
principle /'prɪnsəpl/ *n.* principio
pristine /'prɪstiːn/ *adj.* incontaminato

R

range up /reɪndʒ ʌp/ *v.* elevarsi
reach /riːtʃ/ *v.* raggiungere
renaissance /rɪ'neɪsəns/ *n.* rinascita
require /rɪ'kwaɪər/ *v.* richiedere
riches /'rɪtʃɪz/ *n.* ricchezze
rickets /'rɪkɪts/ *n.* rachitismo
rise /raɪz/ *v.* sorgere
royalties /'rɔɪəltɪz/ *n.* diritti d'autore
rush hour /rʌʃ aʊər/ *n.* ora di punta

S

sales figures /seɪlz 'fɪgərs/ *n.* dati di vendita
set /set/ *v.* tramontare
shade /ʃeɪd/ *n.* ombra
shard /ʃɑːd/ *n.* scheggia
sharp /ʃɑːp/ *adj.* attento, sveglio
sleek /sliːk/ *adj.* elegante
slender /'slendər/ *adj.* esile, slanciato
spire /'spaɪər/ *n.* guglia
spread /spred/ *v.* distribuire
starfish /'stɑːˌfɪʃ/ *n.* stella marina
starve /stɑːv/ *v.* morire di fame
storey /'stɔːrɪ/ *n.* piano di un edificio
sunbathe /'sʌnbeɪð/ *v.* prendere il sole
supplement /'sʌplɪmənt/ *n.* integrazione
supply /sə'plaɪ/ *n.* fornitura
sustainable /sə'steɪnəbl/ *adj.* rinnovabile
swap /swɒp/ *v.* scambiare

T

take off /teɪk ɒf/ *v.* partire
thick /θɪk/ *adj.* spessa
throughout /θruː'aʊt/ *adv.* in tutto
tortoise /'tɔːtəs/ *n.* tartaruga
triple-height /'trɪplhaɪt/ *n.* altezza di tre piani

U

unemployment /ˌʌnɪm'plɔɪmənt/ *n.* disoccupazione
uneventful /ˌʌnɪ'ventfl/ *adj.* senza incidenti
unplug /ʌn'plʌg/ *v.* staccare la spina
UV sun rays /juːviː sʌn reɪz/ *n.* raggi ultravioletti

W

weeping-willow /ˌwiː.pɪŋ'wɪl.əʊ/ *n.* salice piangente
weigh /weɪ/ *v.* pesare
whereas /ˌweər'æz/ *conj.* mentre
wind /waɪnd/ *v.* avvolgere
withstand /wɪð'stænd/ *v.* resistere
woodblock printing /'wʊdblɒk' prɪntɪŋ/ *n.* stampa con matrice in legno
World Heritage Site /wɜːld 'herɪtɪdʒ saɪt/ *n.* patrimonio culturale mondiale
wound /wuːnd/ *n.* ferita